Tony Moore was born in South London in 1940 and evacuated to Cardiff two weeks later where he spent his early childhood.

He migrated to Australia in 1948 with his mother and brother. After tolerating school he seized the medical course at Melbourne University where he had an outstanding academic record. With post-graduate qualifications in surgery and rehabilitation medicine, he wandered to Cambridge University to read literature and philosophy.

A nomad by temperament, he has worked in the United States, United Kingdom and Australia in medical specialities, always striving to demon-strate how medical practice relates to other social, creative and emotional rhythms. These themes were explored in his first book, *The Missing Medical Text: Humane Patient Care*.

He is currently Medical Director at Hampton Rehabilitation Hospital.

He has four adult children and lives and writes in the sanctuary provided by the hills of the Mornington Peninsula.

CRY OF THE
DAMAGED MAN

A PERSONAL JOURNEY
OF RECOVERY

TONY MOORE

Pan Original
PAN BOOKS
LONDON, SYDNEY AND AUCKLAND

First published in Australia 1991 by
Pan Macmillan Publishers Australia, Sydney
This edition published 1992 by Pan Books Ltd,
a division of Pan Macmillan Publishers Limited
Cavaye Place, London SW10 9PG
Associated companies throughout the world

1 3 5 7 9 8 6 4 2

ISBN 0 330 32516 7

Printed in England by Clays Ltd, St Ives plc

For my mother
Her courage and care

Whatever was, has changed
Whatever is, will change

CONTENTS

ACKNOWLEDGEMENTS

My appreciation is expressed to a number of people who read the developing manuscript and assisted its progress with their support and suggestions. They include:

Sally Allmand, doctor; Patricia Baker, physiotherapist; Debbie Beal, nurse; Carol Burton, neuropsychologist; Carolyn Chisholm, medical secretary; Carolyn Chuck, kindergarten teacher; Norma Findlay, ward assistant; Jenny MacDonald, nurse; Pat McConchie, co-patient; Prue Mellor, nurse; Jenny Murray, hospital administrator; Freddie Rowe, volunteer worker; and Pat Strong, psychologist.

Specific thanks are due to Carolyn Chisholm, an exceptional secretary who smoothed some strange spelling; and Fiona Giles, an editor who touched the text with sensitivity.

Finally, special gratitude is due to Jenny Murray, a dear friend who helped to guide an unsteady hand.

PREFACE

What follows may provide support for some people and may unsettle others.

This story, like most of my professional life as a doctor and some of my personal life as a fellow struggler, has been guided by the ideal of trying to assist the achievement of full human potential and the avoidance of human waste. It has been shaped by the belief that all things are interconnected, approximate and changing.

Many people suffer illness, injury, or emotional damage, the consequences of which can affect every aspect of their lives, as well as those of family and friends. The process of recovery involves the challenge of reclaiming damaged capacities, the acceptance of those which have been lost and the joy of exploring new ones. This book reveals my personal experience of that journey.

Mornington Peninsula, 1991

1
ROADSIDE

*Count no mortal happy till
he has passed the final limit
of his life without pain.*

Sophocles

When it happened my first thought was, 'How am I going to explain all of this?'

At that moment it was a very peculiar thought because I had no idea what had happened or why I needed to do any explaining. My brain was stunned and struggled to understand the chaos. I was vaguely aware that the car had disintegrated almost completely, with me in the middle of the mess, but I was unable to shift either my confusion or my legs. For a moment I thought the car had exploded.

My glasses had been smashed from my face so everything beyond my left arm's length—the only limb I could move—was a blur. All the windows were shattered and slivers of glass had sprayed into my hands and face. Both sides of the car were buckled towards me, the right side crushing my chest and shoulder, while the engine was rammed onto my lap breaking both legs and forcing the gear stick through my left calf.

In that savage moment my life was changed.

The first emerging sensation seeped slowly towards me. It is still eerie to remember the absolute effortlessness of that black silence. Nothing sustained it. Everything had stopped.

Then, with almost embryonic delicacy, I felt a tiny touch of movement like the first frail flutter of a baby in a womb.

1

It was the return of my breathing beginning as soundless whispers then swelling into frantic gasps for air.

The moments before the smash had been ordinary: driving to work on a clear day with morning FM radio filling the empty space between my thoughts about work and my selections for the office footy tipping competition.

But there is nothing ordinary about being smashed by a speeding thirty-tonne semitrailer. There is nothing everyday about surviving the body–shattering effects of such an impact. And yet the awesome momentum of that truck as it raced through a red light was symbolic of the power needed to bring my energetic and messy life to a halt.

A siren seemed to be screaming inside my head. There was damage everywhere. Broken bits of my body and the car were twisted together in a gruesome embrace. Nothing would let go. I could not move.

My brain was still working and I said out loud, 'Branches of the internal carotid artery'. It was a sort of private prayer to my sharpening conscious state. As a medical student studying anatomy I had memorised the ten named branches of this main artery to the head. In the years which followed, whenever I wanted reassurance that my brain was working accurately, after a dream, or a drink, or a bump on the head, I would try to remember them.

This time I didn't bother with the details. With profound gratitude I realised that I was alive with an active brain.

I never doubted that I would survive. From the first emerging awareness that followed the impact, after those seconds of galactic darkness, following the exploding tuning fork pitch which penetrated my head with its sickening spinning sensation, during my progressive awareness of the twisted destruction around me, and even after the full extent of my injuries had been explained, I knew that I would live.

It wasn't human arrogance or bravery, or a denial of the dangers I faced. It was a simple knowing. This was not to be the time.

Even before anyone arrived at the wreckage my mind was racing to make sure that I survived. I moved my left arm to feel my neck and back, searching for an injury which would help to explain why I couldn't move or feel my legs. My fingers were shaking with the fear of what they might find. But while

I managed to wriggle my toes inside my shoes, which told me that I had been spared a dreaded paraplegia, my fingers found fresh damage.

Beneath the skin of my neck and chest I could feel the telltale crackle of air which signalled a ruptured lung. I tried to remember every possible complication of this injury. The one which terrified me the most was a tension pneumothorax, where the air leaking from the lung within the chest could pump pressure around the heart and block the flow of blood and air to and from the lungs. I knew that this could kill me quickly. The treatment was easy: to push a tube through the chest wall to let the compressed air out. The only thing I had available was a ball point pen. Using my left hand and teeth to remove the ink fill, I grasped it ready to plunge, wondering if it would snap before stabbing through the skin. It was all so matter of fact: no bravery, no pain, no heroism, just a simple act of clinical preparation to save a life.

Holding a pen must have looked strange to the people who had rushed to the car. A bit early to start writing a memoir of the accident. Or perhaps taking the dedication to paper-work a bit far!

Someone appeared at the passenger side of the wreck and asked if I was all right.

'What the hell has happened?' I gasped at him.

'Big bloody truck ran a red,' he said. 'They got him.'

They got *him*. I tried to speak with the same synthetic calm I used as a surgeon when anything really perilous was happening in the operating theatre. In the wreckage my calmness was a cover for the sheer terror I felt. It wasn't the blood on my hands or face, or the air crackling beneath the skin over my ruptured lung, or the pain as I gasped for breath through a chest of broken ribs, or the futile struggle to wrench both broken legs from beneath the engine. It was none of these.

It was the smell of petrol. I did not want to burn. I could not get out. I pulled and pulled helplessly using the power of my thighs on the clamped legs to get them free. But they were like bad teeth resisting extraction: they cracked and crunched.

A few weeks later I was grateful for the chance to embrace the ambulance driver, who, together with a no-nonsense truckie with big biceps, tattoos and a lot of hair, heaved the engine from my knees with a delicately inserted crowbar. As I lifted my shattered legs from under the crumpled dashboard and shoved them onto what was left of the passenger seat there was no pain. At least not until someone responded to my plea that I could not breathe by reaching inside the car and pushing the back of the driving seat down flat. Then I cried out with panic because I had not realised that the whole right side of my chest was pushed in with a double row of smashed ribs. Lying flat, with my diaphragm pushed up, I could not breathe at all.

'Get me up! Get me out!' I urged with two desperate gasps.

'Stay calm,' said the younger ambulance man.

'Stay nothing,' I hissed with grim intensity. 'Please mate, I'm a doctor, I have subcutaneous emphysema, a pneumothorax, a flail chest and I can't bloody breathe.'

'Oh shit,' he said.

'For Christ's sake,' I pleaded with real concern, 'get me to the Royal Melbourne Hospital quickly.'

They lifted me gently from the wreckage and when I croaked, 'Don't forget my briefcase,' they almost dropped me with laughter.

The peak hour traffic was banked back as far as I could see and as they turned the stretcher around to load me into the ambulance, I saw what was left of the car and nearly retched. There just wasn't enough room left for anyone to fit inside it. Debris was everywhere and all sides of the car were crushed. I didn't see the offending truck or its driver—not then nor in the seconds before it hit me.

The man in the car waiting to turn right from the inside lane did see it coming and watched it strike me. He saw what could have happened to him and was brave enough to act as a court witness months later in spite of his nightmares.

The scars of the smash are still on the road seven years later: two sweeping gouges on the surface. The semitrailer slammed into the side of my car then crushed it into the bitumen before spinning it on into the traffic poles. One of them still leans away from the intersection with its side stripped rust-bare by the grind of raw metal from the car. It is a colourless corner.

Months later, when I could drive, I went back. I drove

across the intersection from every direction, coldly, like a test pilot, precise, proud and vulnerable. It was a private visit. No audience, no applause, everyone else going their motoring ways. I didn't look at anyone and I didn't tell anyone. I drove away knowing nothing had been proved. It contributed nothing.

I still shout at trucks. No-one ever hears me above the massive roar of their engines. I shout, 'Fuck off!' with a hoarse defiance that surprises me. Watch one the next time it rolls up alongside you at the traffic lights. Look at its front steel bar protectors, smell its size. It's worth a shout. My shout is a celebration. I know that whatever controls the larger order of things will never send a second semitrailer to damage me. I am safe from that.

As the ambulance progressed up Elizabeth Street, I knew the injuries were serious. I could feel my brain drifting into dullness. I remember trying to stay conscious, at least until I arrived at the Royal Melbourne Hospital, by anticipating all the landmarks along the way. Lying on my back in the ambulance I saw the Post Office to the left, McGills' Stationery and Ted's Camera Store to the right, Myer's to the left, the Victoria Market to the right and finally the Dental Hospital which told me I was nearly there. These days I rarely have the need to travel up Elizabeth Street.

I was not a good driver. I drove the way I lived. We all do. Read *Zen and the Art of Motorcycle Maintenance*. Just as we leave the impact of the way we drive on our cars we leave the imprint of the way we live on our bodies. Look at the inside of your car, then look at your face.

I was a bad driver. I hurried, I was tired, preoccupied and disregardful. And I will admit that in the decades prior to this smash I had been involved in six minor or major collisions each of which was predominantly my fault, and none of which caused anything but a minor injury to anybody. Ironically, this accident, for which I was completely blameless, almost killed me. It is easy for me to admit that the tiredness in my hands and the tension in my mind had contributed in a general way to my earlier careless driving temperament. To this accident, however, these defects contributed very little.

When the glass doors of casualty shut behind me, I closed my eyes with relief, believing I was safe. The hospital had been my home for almost twenty years during my days as a medical student, junior doctor and surgeon. But nothing in that long apprenticeship had prepared me for what I was to experience during the years of my recovery.

Like a wild animal leaving part of its legs in a trader's trap as the price of its escape, I had survived the metal jaws to face the days ahead.

2
CASUALTY

The words to describe pain
are inaccurate and imprecise.

The nurses had to cut my clothes from me in casualty. They had been clean when I left home. The dark blue cords and the black sweater were taken away and burned.

The shoes, smeared with engine muck, were sent home from the hospital in a brown paper bag. Months later, when I was trying to wear shoes again, I found them in my wardrobe. Inside, hiding like two miserable memories, were my socks crusted with dead blood. I lowered them gently into a rubbish bin and shuddered just a bit.

As they wheeled me into the emergency area I looked around blankly and felt grateful that none of it had anything to do with me. I didn't have to rush to resuscitate anyone or hurry to insert intravenous lines or tubes.

Quite quickly a young doctor, whom I had taught as a medical student, took the first necessary step and, using a local anaesthetic after shaving the hair, put the tube into my chest to help expand the collapsed lung. I wasn't certain if it was inexperience or deference which caused him to be hesitant, but he relaxed when I said, 'You are just about to help save my life with that tube. Go for it, I'm glad I got here and it's you and not me that's doing it.'

He did it easily.

Now the pain really started to bite for the first time. For an hour I had been protected by the body's private response to damage. Millions of years of mammalian adaptation to predators and injury had produced a flood of natural chemicals which helped to protect me from the pain and shock. But now I felt them dilute and ebb as nausea and fear came thrusting at me like the blades of winter waves.

My mind kept hanging onto things. Messages must be sent. People must be phoned. I was able to tell the young doctor my phone numbers for home and work. 'Start by telling them I'm all right. Tell them it's just bones.'

For someone who was about to be trolleyed to the X-ray department to have over twenty fractures and ruptured bruised lungs confirmed, it was almost the truth.

I'm certain that the body knows its own limits. After a long session in X-ray, where films were taken of everything which could have been damaged, I began to feel very agitated and uneasy. 'Could we stop soon?' I pleaded, 'I feel very cold and bit cloudy.'

'Just got the pelvis to do,' came the reply from the radiographer.

I lifted my one working arm and thumped it against both sides of my pelvis. 'It's OK,' I said. 'Nothing is broken there. Let's go. I've had enough.'

He explained he was only doing the job requested on the card, but more from the look of me than my request, he relented. Subsequent X-rays showed that a fractured lumbar vertebrae was lurking deep in my back.

Outside the emergency area I came face to face with Bob Thomas, the accident surgeon on duty for that day. He was a friend and a past colleague. His eyes had seen the X-rays of my chest and they spoke first. 'How are you Boy-O?' he asked.

'Okay, I think,' I said, qualifying my certainty with the concern in his expression.

'We'll have to keep an eye on your chest,' he said in just the sort of calm understatement I would have used. 'Both lungs bruised, right one collapsed with a big flail segment.'

'I'll be OK,' I said with less conviction as I tried unsuccessfully to take a convincing breath and was caught by a pain which was becoming more savage with every word. 'Can we get out of here now? I'm starting to feel very cold.'

'Yes, I agree. You've lost a lot of blood, and there are quite a few bones broken.'

Things which go wrong inside a chest can be big mischief. The heart and lungs are the levers of life. Arms and legs are helpful but without blood and breath you die. Everything was beginning to fade, and when my wife and brother-in-law arrived in the emergency area I wasn't quite convinced by my quip, 'Don't worry, it's only kryptonite which weakens me'.

With very great speed, the system of care swallowed me: drugs, drips, blood transfusions, oxygen, antibiotics, catheters, central pressure lines, anaesthetics, operations, screws, plasters, tubes, respirators, morphine and gentle, skilled hands.

Simply put, the staff of the Royal Melbourne Hospital saved my life.

3
INTENSIVE CARE

Now o'er the one half-world
Nature seems dead, and wicked dreams abuse
The curtain'd sleep.

Shakespeare

I was spared the sort of terrors suffered by those who wake up in the intensive care ward without knowing why or how they got there, or what was being done to them. From the look on my surgeon's face I knew that was where I would be taken following the operations, and I knew most of what to expect.

The first day or two were very dim and I had a dwindling ability to link myself to anything. I couldn't even dream properly. It was all adrift.

My first real awareness was the loudness of the radio on the nursing sister's control desk, and the incessant heave of its rhythms. Perhaps it helped them to work with the horrors they had to care for. But the smash had damaged my hearing and the sounds seemed too loud and were joined to a shrill ringing in my ears.

I was in no position to make a polite request for them to turn the music down. I had tried to tell them through mute gestures that the endotracheal tube linking me to the respirator was partially dislodged out of my windpipe into my throat. It's a bit hard to swallow something that is choking you from within. Eventually, they took the tube out but said it would need to be replaced. I gruffed I didn't want it back, so they

10

conceded that they would leave it out for a few hours and then measure how well my crushed chest had moved oxygen into the damaged lungs. I breathed brilliantly for hours even though the broken ribs hurt badly. It worked, and the tube stayed out. 'Clinically much improved post extubation,' said the medical notes.

But while the tube was in its misplaced position it bruised my vocal cords, so for weeks I could only whisper. It was hard to speak with sustained softness without becoming exhausted very quickly. And worse, in the following weeks, it was impossible to shout at all without any volume in my voice. Apart from the radio noise, there was nothing I needed to raise my voice about in intensive care. I watched the ebb and flow of the staff and their skills with complete trust and admiration.

On the afternoon of the third day I was drifting in the peace and pleasures of pethidine, slipping to and from the sort of artificial sleep where half dreams can be touched, when, through a haze of softness, a nurse seemed to float towards me. Her face was like a young Geraldine Chaplin and her hands moved my pillows and touched my arm. Her clothes were white, her face angelic and her tiny touch so delicate. If by some rare decision I had arrived in heaven, at that moment I would not have cared.

Two other nurses joined her and one whispered, 'Time for a wash'. They worked like a ballet corps in slow motion, softly moving me forwards, to the side, sponging, touching, towelling with clean tenderness, and when one gently washed my genitals I felt nothing but the compassion of her care in knowing what a humiliating ordeal this whole mess was for me. Perhaps she sensed what I was to face in the months ahead because her responses seemed to show that she knew an accident could both smash open a body and break open a life.

The appearance of some of the other patients in intensive care disturbed me. They were surrounded by the cloud of death. The medical me knew I could not 'catch' death but I was relieved when the staff told me I would be moved into the open ward soon.

4
THE WARD

*It is the helplessness of illness
which is humiliating.*

I wish I could find a way to help all treating staff in every
hospital understand the horrible sense of abandonment which
patients feel when they are shifted from a familiar site to a
strange one, or when they are left exposed and unattended
in any place around the hospital.

Perhaps it was tiredness or tension or pain, but when I
was moved from intensive care to the general ward I felt desolate.
The delay in the shift and the isolation when I was left alone
for some time in the corridor made me feel as though my
life's support system had been ripped away. I had a similar
sense of abandonment later on during a long delay in the X-
ray department and broke down completely when I was simply
transferred from one ward room to another.

When the link to life seems tenuous the immediate world
is clung to desperately. That world became my ward room.
I had a passionate need to make that corner of the world
a home because I knew my stay would be a long one. Posters
of forests, photos, cards, flowers and fruit were a help. But
it was the love of my family and friends and the care of the
staff which was provided in that small space which helped most
to shift the direction of damage towards recovery.

For twenty years I had worked at the Royal Melbourne

Hospital and I was grateful for the protection my single room gave me from the numerous, well-intentioned visits from the staff. The new nurse who resented my 'privileged' status wasn't to know how many cups of coffee I had needed in the surgeon's tea room at two am during those decades. I was just grateful to be cared for by people who had my total trust.

Although it provided essential protection and privacy, the room was also full of constraints. I could not move. People were gone. Human links and the luxury of availability were lost.

My sense of isolation and abandonment was reduced by a discovery I made during the early days in the ward. I noticed there was a telephone connection on the skirting board of one of the walls and I managed to get an old phone from home brought in and connected. This link to a lost world helped my peace of mind. Patients who have the most severe illnesses or injuries are the ones usually placed in the single rooms, but they are also the ones most likely to have the conflicting needs of solitude for rest and company for support. The telephone was a wonderful compromise which allowed some freedom for a patient in isolation. I could ring my mother and family to see how they were and to reduce my anxiety about their well-being, and I could speak to friends.

All doctors dread the sound of the telephone, it rarely brings good news. Night calls, someone in distress, someone damaged—its messages often seem to have a wilful purpose to destroy sleep and peace. Even today when a phone rings during a film, in a shop or in someone else's home, I feel myself tense. But during the early weeks in hospital its role changed. I could only use it to ring out and it provided a lifeline rather than a wire around the neck of my peace. It was a perfect aid to convalescence during the day and early evening, even though it could not help me through the tormenting hours before dawn.

Each person suffers in their own way but on one thing all those who have endured major damage agree: the nights provide the most terrifying moments. A cruel type of tiredness forms a grim gang with physical exhaustion and pain. There is no protection at two am: no people, no business, no diversions, no buoyancy, no dreams.

Dawn provides some release from this terror. During the

early hours I looked in the shaving mirror and saw a pair of bruised eyes blackened by the blows of a sleepless night. During the first eight weeks after the accident I lost over three stone in weight and more than three hundred hours of sleep. And while people noticed one, they knew little of the other. They all saw the bad temper of trashy tiredness but only a few understood my total exhaustion.

Sometimes humans cope with calamity better than they manage minor irritations, particularly when the cause of the exasperation is someone interfering with a necessary routine. Matters of personal care became especially important to me in the ward. Whereas before the accident I could go happily without shaving on the weekend or holidays, afterwards I could not bear to be scruffy in that way. It related to the discipline of the hospital. Shaving was one small task I could manage which produced a clean result. It had to be done because it could be done and because it was a positive contribution to my otherwise fragmented appearance. Shaving, sponging, clean sheets, clean bedgown and fresh pillowslips all helped to prevent feelings of neglect and decline. I thought about people in trenches and detention camps. Their humanity was partly broken down by enforced dirtiness.

In the ward, simple tasks done in a routine way helped me to reclaim some order from chaos. Shaving and sponging were essential to my early morning ritual. They were eventually thwarted by a lazy night nurse who, because he thought he was doing the day staff's duties, refused to bring me towels and a wash basin at five am as the other night nurses had done willingly before the morning hand-over. He probably thought I was being a 'demanding nuisance', or 'unreasonable' or 'off my head'.

Even though I was spared a direct head injury, my brain didn't work efficiently in the early weeks. I knew I was tired but it was more than fatigue and weariness. I had difficulty with concentration and memory. The latter upset me because it is very difficult to be infallible when your memory is gone! I could not remember people's names, things I had to do, authors, books I had read, and I couldn't worry the memory loose as I had before the accident. At least this loss of my sense of certainty helped reduce the relentless dogmatism which had previously afflicted my conversations.

Perhaps my mental cloudiness was due to the struggle my lungs were having to provide enough oxygen for my brain. I had a respirator assist machine beside my bed and used it as I had been instructed, ten minutes in each hour. It self-triggered from my breathing and helped to expand the lungs to prevent their collapse and the development of pneumonia. I knew exactly why I had to use it, but I wondered how many other patients didn't persist with the intense pain of moving crushed ribs because they hadn't had the benefits explained. In spite of my efforts I still had an episode of severe pleuritic pain during the first week in the ward. It was associated with some collapse of the right lung, a temperature and coughing blood.

I tried to get my mind off the details of the damage by reading. All my life I had been partnered by books and yet I couldn't read the volumes carefully chosen by friends as bedside gifts. I didn't have the energy needed to open them and it felt like I was turning my back on close friends: so many of the writers could have helped me. But my power to concentrate even for a short time had been ripped away. During the early days in the ward my eyes just slid along the line and off the edge of the page. Sometimes, when it was near dawn, and I had some frail early morning energy, I would try to remember fragments of passages which had previously given me strength:

Seneca's question: 'What is the finest part you have played?'

Coleridge's quote: 'A man who has thought about the human state should be pessimistic, but the only spirit compatible with human dignity is optimism'.

And a Spanish proverb which helped more than any: 'All the darkness in the world cannot extinguish the light from a solitary candle'.

It didn't matter that my memory of them was incomplete or inaccurate, or that I could not always remember their author. I gained support from their spirit. The fact that I could recall even fragments of them was reassuring and helped to sustain me to a stage where I managed to read a book.

The first book I tried to read to completion had been given to me by a night charge nurse, Rae Lockie, who I had known for twenty years and who, through quietly caring observation, selected just the thing I needed to read. It was the story of the unprecedented courage and endurance of Mawson in *This Accursed Land*. It created a yearning in me for adventure and for marathon treks to strange, unseen territories in all areas of existence. I had a passion to experience everything which was still beyond me. And I knew I would have to leave my administrative position working in the Health Department as soon as I was well enough. Beginning in the earliest days of my recovery, the accident was changing the way I viewed the world, as well as my body.

I couldn't finish the book because my left arm, the only limb I could use to hold it, developed a severe inflammation in the vein due to the irritation caused by the necessary but numerous drugs flowing into the intravenous line.

At the end of the first week in the ward I had no voice, all four limbs out of action, my brain numb with tiredness and pain, and my spirit struggling through enforced isolation. Things could not get worse. But they did.

The most intensely humiliating moment of the whole ordeal of recovery was symbolic of the total helplessness I felt during my early bedfast days in hospital. With my bowels blocked by days of pethidine and my legs cased in plasters, I was left suspended on a hoist over a commode. The efforts of toilet caused both thighs to cramp under the plasters and my abdominal muscles to join them in a sickening spasm. The anguish of the cramps was worse than the pain caused by the original fractures. But neither was as bad as the total physical and emotional humiliation I felt during those moments. I was left to impotently press a non-responding call button and to 'shout' for help with a whisper for a voice.

When the nurse finally came, I had almost passed out with the pain. A moment later one of my closest medical friends came to the door. 'Please go away, Dick,' I whispered, with tears breaking over my face.

5
VISITORS

Loneliness is not a longing for company,
It is a longing for kind.

Marilyn French

Visitors came. Some simply left messages or spoke to the nurses without disturbing me. There were friends, work mates, consultants, young doctors, colleagues in administration, nurses from the past, friends from the kitchen and cleaning staff and interpreters, all expressing a concern which helped to resuscitate my spirits. I was so grateful.

Sometimes the visitors' messages went astray and I learned afterwards of the feelings they had expressed. While I was upset that their good wishes were lost in the relay, I understood and appreciated that the ward staff were protecting me by not encouraging visitors during the early weeks. What surprised me about visitors was this: some I expected to visit didn't, a few I wanted to come stayed away, and those I did not expect to see, arrived.

As I lay forced flat on my back in bed I realised hospital visits were motivated by multiple and complex human emotions. There was a marked randomness in who came and when, how long they stayed, and what they wanted. Some were dutiful, almost incidental visits. Others had an abstract curiosity. A few were just gossipy; and happily only one or two were insensitive. Most were generated by feelings of friendship and I felt the tenderness of their affection.

The visitors I liked the best came unexpectedly and occasionally after nine pm at night. Some of them were frequent callers.

John Forbes a doctor friend, was positive, energetic, reliable, thoughtful, entertaining, perhaps professionally lonely and occasionally exhausting. Bess McRae a work partner, was caring, protective, affectionate and kind. Jim Carson was a surprise: warm, perceptive, patient, and intrigued, a puzzle—I hadn't known him very well at work before the accident. Tom Allmand my father-in-law was loyal, diverting and considerate. Sue Stoyles was a good mate and fun. A close friend Jenny Murray felt every pain I suffered. Pat Strong a life-long confidante was understanding and helped so much.

Peter De Grant was the easiest company, abstract, brotherly, understated, non-intrusive and gentle—a fascinated and facilitating partner. He was the only one who continued to call regularly well after I was strong enough to return home. He was a healing partner. And when, seven months on, I took the first truly strong steps, his visits vanished.

The visits I disliked the most were those in the early days from people who were seeking strength from me. Some who visited to help themselves were not so much parasitic as just hopelessly inappropriate.

Some people, perhaps well-meaning, behaved in a way which said—if you are awake in the ward you are available. In they came with their bodies led by the noise of their voices. I am not ashamed to say I soon learned how to foil them. I feigned sleep. They would open the ward room door, look in, shuffle sounds to see if I was awake, and then depart. They didn't appreciate the importance of both sleep and rest in recovery.

The worst of them were the ones who assaulted me with their troubles. I was seen as a securely immobile and sympathetic target with the time and opportunity to help them solve their problems. At that time I barely had the energy needed to survive each day.

There was one sort of person who particularly hindered recovery. These were the people who were predominantly precautionary, defensive, doubting, suspicious and fearful. Their characteristics were all negative. Contact with them could draw me into a futile pattern of attempting to relieve their anxieties. But I never could, for in the place of the resolved doubt another appeared. In the place of an existing worry an ever bigger concern emerged. I would feel drawn into an ever-expanding and accelerating treadmill in trying to overcome their sequential problems. It was a wearing and exhausting task and, when my energy needed to be spent on survival, I could not afford to waste it trying to allay the intractable anxieties of others.

These people had to be told, 'At this stage of my healing you must seek your support elsewhere. Your needs are sucking the life blood from my body.'

They had to be firmly told to go away. Why do some people presume that a patient must be bored in hospital? For me healing was a full-time job with compulsory overtime every night and weekend. The time of recovery was not spent in idle relaxation. There was big work to be done to achieve physical recovery and even bigger work to resuscitate the spirit.

I was almost defeated by the limited insight of some visitors who claimed to care but who did not understand that healing had first call on the reserves of energy available to a severely injured patient. My body jealously guarded its depleted resources of energy and resisted all attempts to squander it on anything but its survival and recovery. For those people who trespassed on my limited reserves, there was little hope. As Dr Samuel Johnson said, 'The cure for a lack of insight presumes the cure'.

While I was in the ward a medical colleague I admire as a lovely doctor asked me genuinely, 'From what you have been through so far what is the most important new thing you've learned in relation to caring for patients?'

Without hesitation I replied, 'The importance of rest to recovery'.

It was an intense appreciation of the relationship between rest and the energy needed for recuperation.

Nevertheless, it is a reality of hospital care that patients with the most severe medical problems have a corresponding need for the most frequent visits by staff. Some, like the nurse who came to remove the stitches from my face, or the specialist who set up the bedside respirator, had a specific task to do. Others, including the doctors, nurses and physiotherapists, called frequently during the day to assess my progress and to make any necessary adjustments to the treatment. And there was an additional legion of staff including ward assistants, orderlies, cleaners, food services staff, blood sisters, volunteers, newsboys, kiosk ladies, delivery people and chaplains—all with jobs to do.

These people, and most of their visits, were necessary. But the lack of any coordination in the timing of their calls made it almost impossible to get a single uninterrupted hour during the day.

Additional visitors who were unnecessary or unsupportive were totally unwelcome.

Those visitors who had a well-intentioned desire for my day to be fully occupied did not appreciate how long it took to do ordinary things. Most people with disabilities would prefer not to be given help or sympathy, but the time to do tasks for themselves free of takeovers and interfering assistance. You do not take a crayon from a child simply because you feel you can draw a better picture. Everyone recovering from major injuries tries to learn how to cope with their difficulties and regain their capacities. These lessons take time. Visitors who offered unwarranted assistance or advice were like those who helped someone to cheat in an exam: in trying to help them pass one event they were increasing the chances of them failing their life.

Visitors who had a real understanding of the ordeals of recovery didn't interfere. They noticed things and complemented the natural flow of recovery with their insight. They saw that the respirator was disconnected and knew the worries about my chest were less. They noticed the bag was gone from the bedside and were glad for me that the catheter had been removed. They didn't bring food or fruit until the intravenous line had been taken out. They brought soft music tapes and left without imposing long chats. They didn't ask me if I wanted anything. They brought what they felt I needed. They looked into my eyes and knew how I felt without asking.

For close family and friends, hospital visits could be a source of great stress. As a patient preoccupied with my survival, I'm ashamed to say I paid only passing attention to the trials they had to endure.

Almost everyone who visits a severely ill family member or close friend feels an increasing sense of tension as they set out on their journey to the hospital. Why do the traffic lights always seem to turn red as they approach? Why is the traffic always heavy or the road soaked with rain? How will the patient be: better or with some new complication? How much should

I try to help? What should I say? What will be his mood today? Should I tell him about some problem at home?

At the end of a tiring day, when the added stress and work in the household has taken its toll, visiting can be demanding. A visitor can never anticipate whether a patient will be emotionally fidgety and restless at the cruelty of his restraint, or whether his grumpiness will express itself as tedious quibbling.

Improvement and recovery always produces a flood of relief for the visitor because there is a level of anxiety over someone's wellbeing which is beyond love and is a fight against real fear.

I tried very hard to make my four children's first visit to see me in hospital gentle and happy. I think it went well. They were frightened by not knowing what to expect and I was relieved that I had enough buoyancy on that day to be bright and 'usual'. But I think they were alarmed to see how their indestructible dad looked after the days in intensive care and the first days in the ward. They brought up pizzas and watched 'Countdown' on a tiny television. It was like transferring the home to the hospital and helped them to cope with the horror of what had happened.

Over the next week or two their Sunday night visits became difficult. They were bored. Six people in a small room was suffocating and they were restless. I was tired at the end of the day and there were too many for too long so I was glad to recover some peace when I was alone.

As I got stronger I felt a deep appreciation of the gestures the children made. They showed imagination and care at an age when neither are common: thoughtful questions, considerate help, and funny presents. And I was moved by their anxiety on my behalf.

With time to reflect in the hospital, it hurt when I felt the inadequacies of my fatherhood. Busy, achieving, over-committed and preoccupied fathers who care about their children can still neglect them. To make excuses would simply mask the love I feel for them.

But it must have been difficult for the children. They wanted me to be well so much that I had to be brave, yet I wasn't brave enough to ask them what was in their thoughts. During the first week all but one wrote me a little note expressing their feelings and trying to hide their fears. One couldn't write.

He was shaken when he saw me in hospital and that night asked his mother, 'Will Dad die?'

Children want their fathers well. Partly for his sake and also for theirs. The wish for parents to be available and strong is one of the reasons why children accelerate the recovery ahead of the reality and why they blot out painful events. Another is that they wish to avoid what they feel are the undesirable social stains of having a disabled father. Partly it is due to the simple self-orientation of adolescence. Whatever the reasons, at all stages, they had me recovered beyond my state. And there is a basic incompatibility between the exuberance of four young teenagers and the mood caused by tiredness and depletion.

Surviving, I continued trying to improve my fragmented fatherhood. The experience helped me to understand my children a little better; and I began to solve the puzzle of why, with an almost totally reliable memory for other things, I have very few recollections of my own fatherless childhood.

The children could not understand the natural seep-stain of blood on my leg plasters. They complained to their mother that Dad was not being looked after properly in the hospital. With her practised care and patience she explained that the stains were usual in a first plaster put on a fracture when the skin and muscles had been damaged or operated on. The explanation may have helped them, but she still encouraged me to ask the nurses for bandages to cover those shifting maps of crimson concern.

During the earliest days of my ward care, before the raw, irrational rage of suffering took hold, I felt a profound sense of gratitude to my wife Sally for the love and loyalty she had spent on me when my life was a compost of emotional confusion.

Her direct trust deserved more than the 'cleverness' I imposed on everything; and her steady, sound companionship should have been reciprocated with better support. While I cannot lacerate myself with regret or remorse about the past, I can relate a heartfelt regard for the largely unrequited emotional effort she gave to our partnership in those times of my emerging sanity. There is a sepia sadness in my memory of those years. Perhaps it is of little consolation that if my approach to her was less than perfect during those decades, the care I gave myself was even worse.

During my lowest moments of recovery in hospital, when my inner being ached more than my bones, I was convinced that my approach to life had gone some way to killing her spirit and that the added stresses of the accident and its consequences were sent to damage anything which still survived. Later on, when I was unable to heal myself within, I felt she could have wished me gone with justification. But I survived and so did she and we try to treat each other decently.

To be a wife to me in those decades when I was driven by demons of personal relevance was a task beyond any woman. I appreciate that during those times she was mostly for me, and I am partially nourished by the belief that I did not run from my basic responsibilities.

I wonder if there is a simple obligation on each of us to bare ourselves as being better than we are, for our moral ideals always seem to exceed our moral performance. And if self-deception is the way we usually cope, perhaps honesty just might be easier.

For me to tell the whole story of how the accident and its consequences affected the family would be like putting them in a car and running a truck through them. Some experiences and memories are too private to share. They have been bruised enough.

When my mother came to visit she wasn't overawed by the technology or displaced by the experts. Orphaned at five, a single parent at thirty, always in a foreign land, she responded as she had survived. 'Don't dwell, don't despair, do what needs to be done.'

Her small, strong hands massaged my toes beyond the plasters and the pain beyond my legs.

What a simple debt I owe her. She has been a universe of unvarying strength. Perhaps I have inherited a touch of her indestructibility. And now that the simple richness of her mind is betrayed by a disintegrating memory, I can care for her. I feel humbled and honoured by the mission.

At my request she brought me string bags full of oranges and mandarins. The body must know its own business, otherwise how can I explain this: before the accident I loved to eat apples and was indifferent to the messy delights of oranges or other finger soaking peelers. But during recovery I craved citrus fruit. It had something my body knew I needed. Was it potassium, vitamins, or a special sort of sugar? Now, like an overripe fallen fruit, they have done their job and retired. Today I can be found at a market stall looking gratefully at oranges remembering how they helped my bones to heal, but buying apples and pears and bananas to take home.

I had no appetite for most of the food which came to the ward. But one of the sweetest moments of recovery came when a friend arrived at the door of my room and simply said without even a hello, 'What would you like more than anything in the world?'

'A lobster salad,' I said.

Two hours later, without fuss, this splendid delight was smuggled into the ward and that night I slept soundly for several hours covered with a blanket of gratitude.

This joy was almost matched by the pleasure I felt when a friend brought me a bottle of Baileys Irish Cream. First-class fuel for winter. Mother's milk for men—and the night nurses didn't mind a nip either. Looking back, I couldn't remember it ever having been mentioned in any therapeutic text book. The astonishing ignorance of the medical profession!

There are quite a few things like that which are missing from today's formal texts. Music is one and being held is another. And the most important of all is the need to capture the gypsy will to recover. It wanders in a nomadic way sometimes difficult to find and always difficult to retain. Without this vagabond as a partner I knew it would be a greater struggle to overcome my distress.

I had some friends who couldn't grieve aloud. There was no public face to their sorrow and yet their fears and sadness were as real as those whose concerns were on open show. Their private wish for me to recover was silenced by the consideration that 'it was better not to visit'. In my damaged state there was little I could do about these restrictions. Ward voyeurs could come and go. People could arrive and ride on my convalescence leaving me weary and used. But my forbidden friends who sent silent prayers and promises helped me to heal. Their goodness is built into my bones.

Human warmth is a form of nutrition. It is not so much who you have regard for but who and what you are when you are with them which matters most.

6
'WRITE IT DOWN'

*Writing helps to prevent the flaw of having
one truth for conversation, and another for life.*

One visitor who had special significance was a doctor friend, Douglas Dowling, who visited me in the ward and said, 'You should write it all down'.

That was about five weeks after the smash. I barely had the energy to exist. Watching television was sapping, talking to people tired me totally and reading drained my nerves. I only wanted to rest or, on good days, listen to gentle music.

'Later, perhaps,' I replied without conviction or intent.

'You might forget all the details,' he pressed.

'Then perhaps they are better forgotten.'

I was positively repelled by the idea of doing it. All I wanted was for the whole horrible experience to go away, to reach tomorrow and not dwell on yesterday.

The next week he was back again. 'I've got some note-pads and some pencils.'

I responded with a pleading look which said—why are you doing this to me?

'Writing has always given you pleasure. Treat yourself.'

'It will give me no pleasure,' I held out stubbornly.

'Then it might help some of the many others who have suffered in a smash,' he paused, 'or their families and friends.' He pressed on, 'Or the many health professionals who need help in understanding what their patients go through'.

'But it's not the physical side of things which is the battle,' I said.

'Then write about the other things. Show everyone the real things which all accident victims suffer. You are in an ideal position. You're a doctor, you're going through it as a patient, and you can write. Just start. Show how your accident is part of the larger event of your life.'

So I started, not on his notepads, but on scrappy bits of notepaper, in scribbles on the inside of book covers, on scruffy pieces of memory, and on a driving desire to share the truth.

When I began I wasn't sure if I could achieve any of what he expected. For me the honest purpose of the notes was simply to complete a few more jigsaw pieces in the puzzle of a life, and more importantly, perhaps to help prevent some human waste.

One thing is certain, I know I am not alone in the sentiments set out in these pages. Although many of my trauma patients and others of whom I know nothing have experienced them in their own way, I have neither the desire nor the right to breach their trust with any details of their personal suffering. These notes simply set out my experience of a single accident.

I know they sound seriously self-orientated. That is not because of my extravagant ego but because the heart of the emotional experience of road trauma is that the damage suffered to the body and spirit is intensely personal. For people who have not been seriously injured some of this may sound like soft nonsense. They have never travelled this road. Maybe that provides a greater reason to go forwards and help them understand some of the ordeals which confront all accident victims.

Some patients write about their silent sensations and perhaps many more should. The writing of a never-to-be-sent letter which unfolds deep human frustrations or ulcerating anger, or which describes a profound sadness it is too late to speak, can ease personal sufferings for which no solutions are apparent.

7
EARLY EMOTIONS

Freedom's just another word
for nothin' left to lose

Kris Kristofferson

It was about this time, some weeks after the smash, when I had stopped trying to be so successful at getting better and when the energy needed to keep the inner wretchedness away had become too exhausting, that I began to feel the whole of what the accident had done to me. I stopped saying I was 'OK'.

It happened slowly and caused more harm than if the feelings of physical violation had been allowed to emerge at their own time. I had ruthlessly restrained their expression and couldn't let myself ease these restrictions until my shaken mind was certain I had done an uncompromisingly perfect job on my physical recovery. I had believed that this brittle bravado was essential for my restoration.

It's of small support for me now to admit how mistaken was my desperate conviction that, being so depleted internally, any attempt to progress on more than one clearly-focused front was beyond me. At that time, there was a profound yet foolish fear that if I slowed down to let my feelings catch up to partner my physical healing, the whole road to recovery would crumble under limping steps. The force of my denial was matched only by the ferocity of the feelings when they tore themselves free and demanded their day.

The accident caused an alteration which involved a quite

unnerving primary change. It produced the unsettling sensation that I had been forced to become something different from what I was, and, more strangely, that I was both the spectator and the subject of the change. Much later I wondered if this was how an assault or rape victim might feel.

At first it was like a dream. You reach out and try to grasp the experience but your hands go right through its essence. Something is missing. The event is clear but the process is blurred. The blunt 'what' of the event is there but the diffuse 'why' is missing. So is the meaning of it. Then, gradually, you feel the full pain of change and rage at its intrusion. Nothing is what it was. You feel alien to yourself. Your sensations and responses are those of an uninvited internal stranger. When the alteration starts you actually watch it happening like a voyeur on your own emotions; then, frighteningly, the window becomes a mirror and with it the realisation that you cannot move without the stranger shifting too.

The accident pushed me sideways but the consequences knocked me flat. When I looked down at my emotional self I saw something foreign. I had been changed from someone who acted on the world, who pressed, influenced, shaped, moulded and altered small parts of it, to one who had been acted on by its forces. The doer had been done: the worst of him had become the victim.

I was distressed by the feeling that the person I had been no longer existed. He had become passive, truce-seeking and conciliatory. I felt a primordial sense of indignation that the guiding fates had abandoned me. Years passed before I understood that the accident was an inevitable event in the journey of my life.

'You were lucky you weren't killed,' they said kindly in the early weeks.

I wanted to scream at them, 'I was!'

In a way I felt a sense of death. The person they saw was not the human they once knew. But I held my tongue. People did not want to hear introspective indulgence from a lucky survivor. They wanted to hear what I feel now, after seven years, as I live each moment with gratitude.

But in the ward there was the beginning of an eroding despair where life was restricted physically and emotionally to the limit of what could be called an existence. At those moments

I believed that I had not been destined to survive the accident and that my continuity was just a mocking cruelty. I felt as though my own emotions had been removed and substituted with something bland. My vigour and audacity, my humour and sensuous joy, and the wonderful exhilaration I felt with extremes of effort were all gone. So was that minute and delicate joy I felt when chasing new thoughts: the perfect thrill of touching the details of my curiosity. Not much of the primary me was left. During those early months I felt that the being who remained was destined to live a life in limbo, free of extremes, of pleasure, and of that rich sadness through which I had occasionally gained some awareness.

I had always believed that individuals who enjoyed sustained good fortune during the early part of their lives had better be on guard later on. I suppose I had it coming, but it was the size and swiftness of the changes enforced by the accident which were beyond me rather than their nature. They were unmanageably rapid. Perhaps the changes would have arrived in time but without the supersonic ferocity which was so damaging.

At its worst I felt the sense of alteration had insinuated through my total being. Nothing was left untouched: my energy, my body, my spirits, emotions, pleasures, sense of fun, will, and the private things which mattered—all were trespassed and trampled.

When I felt most despondent, there was a frightening sense of stillness, a sensation that I was outside immediate events and beyond everyday occurrences. There was a void—a loss of the sensations of pleasure and discomfort. It felt as though the life I was living 'in' was not my own and that I had been forced to have an unwanted social and emotional transplant.

At those moments there was a sensation that someone or something else occupied my body: feelings and responses were alien. Perhaps those around me felt the changes were an improvement and that I had become more as they wished me to be, but at that time I did not really care how they felt or what they thought.

It is possible that impoverished sleep and medical drugs contributed to those feelings of alteration, but I know in my heart they were a form of mute anger and inarticulate indignation: the silent humiliating rage of the slave. I had lost the capacity to determine those events which were my basic right, simple everyday things which one takes for granted such as when to sleep, wake, eat, rest, talk, laugh, move, wash, isolate, move away, engage, work, dispute, create and cuddle.

Thankfully it didn't last. That time was just one dark layer in the geology of my life. Perhaps an emotional dig at some future time will reveal all the strata. The layers of the events in that earlier life will never be lost: seams of sorrow, joy and pain; broad bands of numbing stability; black lines of unhappiness, and flint sharp strikes of excitement are all there buried beneath the enriched years which have followed. Occasionally a memory or an event will cause the internal forces to shift and the covering crust to crack. Then the seams of pain can show again—but they are lifeless fossils. I can look at them with detachment. They do not hurt like the time when they were the whole raw surface of existence.

Although it was a bitter struggle to cope with the restraints and restrictions I did not fight against being a patient. In particular, I did not project my anger onto the medical staff, a response which seems to be common to the point of being tedious in many accounts of the experience of illness: the uncommunicative, insensitive doctors, the peremptory ward nurse, or the bungling administrator were stereotypes I encountered very rarely.

I knew the staff had a job to do and for them to concentrate on those tasks with intensity and accuracy often created an impression of professional remoteness. I didn't mind if I was treated as a mass of broken bones and injuries. That is what I was and that was where I wanted their skills to focus.

At no time during the recovery did I want to be my own doctor. While there were many moments when the medical Tony gained new insights or a fresh emphasis about doctorship—such as the necessity of rest, the separate timing of physical and emotional recovery, the importance of human friendship, and other thoughts along the journey—I understood the wisdom of the established medical tradition that doctors should not become involved with the treatment of themselves or their loved ones.

Aside from the issue of basic professional courtesy, the axiom 'the doctor who treats himself or herself has a fool for a patient' is true in relation to both emotional involvement and perspectives of judgment. There is a great difference between a doctor who is a patient trying to use medical knowledge in a self-treating way on the one hand, and using that medical insight to strengthen a commitment to getting better as a patient on the other.

Beginning right from the first moments in the emergency area, I tried to avoid involving myself in the tasks which were the doctor's responsibility. Michael Mullerworth, the thoracic surgeon who came to casualty to direct my chest injury management, began to explain what was going to be done. I felt he was treating me with extravagant courtesy and that the extensive details he was relating were a concession to my medical status. I was also very jittery about the increasing difficulty I was having with my breathing.

'Please Michael,' I said. 'Do what you need to do, but please get on with it. I trust your judgment and skill absolutely. Whatever you decide is fine.'

Fortunately, I was spared complications from any of the injuries and numerous operations and procedures carried out on me because of both the skills of those caring for me, and, more importantly, my total trust in their ability. I did not worry myself into complications or slow healing through distrust. A distrustful patient can project that doubt onto the treating staff and can affect both the medical treatment and its outcome.

People said it must have been awful being a doctor and a patient. It wasn't. In terms of medical awareness it was almost entirely an advantage. But there was one exception. It was not easy to find someone to talk to about my fears. Most of the doctors caring for me were friends, past teachers or students, and I trusted their skills. I could talk to them about medical matters but not about my internal suffering. The fault was mine, for they were available had I been courageous enough to share my sorrows.

When the journey into feelings began, it initially followed the same self-contained and stoic patterns as my physical endeavours. With gradual awareness I admitted many things to myself long before I was able to share them with others. I behaved like an unconscious patient regaining his senses. I watched the world, particularly the world within, before I let anyone know that I had gained the sight to see the deeper damage.

There were times during my early recovery when I treated

myself with kindness and generosity. But they did not balance the moments when I minced myself up with a wilful madness which crushed my desire to provide the care I deserved. My disregard was like the unsettlingly nebulous anger of adolescence. It had a life of its own which was totally devoid of a concern for consequences. Without clear cause, it was bewildering; and without discretion, it directed itself towards any bystander who tried even well-intentioned interference.

One such unfortunate soul was a social worker who arrived unannounced, with good intentions in one hand and 'understanding' in the other. She asked me if there was anything I needed. I made a graceless and bawdy reply. Not surprisingly she didn't come back and I achieved my prickly purpose with a comment which ensured she would not bother me any more. Pathetic really, because I desperately needed someone to talk to.

This was also the case with a woman who came to interview me some time later for her formal study on how doctors cope with their illnesses. It was impossible for me to be emotionally open with her. I did my best with bluff and bravado to show her I had just shrugged the whole thing off. She obviously sensed the size of the fortress around my feelings but could not find a way in. Her record of that interview, which she kindly sent to me at my request when I began to write seriously about my recovery, was sharply accurate: 'Blank expression, disturbingly penetrating gaze, contrived and controlled presentation'.

Her visit came at one of those times during my recovery when I was at war with everything around me and was certain I would be crushed. My emotions would change instantaneously and without any regard for the moment. It upset me when the wildcat union of my spirits went on strike. Without warning, without discussion, without negotiation, they would down tools and walk off the job taking my happiness and harmony with them. Later on, I conceded that their conditions had been in need of some improvement for a long, long time. Perhaps my self-deceiving ways had contributed to an unsympathetic management style for too long. At least the smash forced me to negotiate a better way of managing my moods.

But no one should underestimate the intensity of the indignation and anger felt by road accident victims. It never really departs. There was a persistent background static of subdued agitation behind everything which related to my surrounding world. An irritation intruded unfairly into my personal judgments of events and people. It felt as though my capacity for fairness had been diverted away from a generous consideration of others towards an indulgent consideration of myself. But I could no more command the irrationality to go away than I could have ordered diarrhoea to stop.

I am certain that those who have suffered major injuries are not always good company. They can seem remote, pre-occupied, agitated, indignant and angry for no obvious reason. But there is an unfathomable and unmanageable secret reason within them and it burns like a fire in a petrol depot, erupting randomly into destructive explosions. It is mute rage.

If to the incendiary effects of this angry arsonist one adds the reduced emotional resilience which afflicts the sufferer, one begins to understand the ingredients which can contribute to this appalling state of emotional unpredictability. On some days even the most minor irritations cannot be coped with.

Everyone living in Australia has experienced those hot humid days when suffocating winds seem to sere us and roast our throats. Exhausted, we silently sweat ourselves out, ready to snap at others as our energy and enthusiasm are depleted. For those recovering from massive injuries, days, weeks and months of unrelieved human humidity can go by while our spirits wait for the cool change of restoration. If it is delayed there can be days of fearful turbulence when real doubts arise that calmness will ever return. Then the sufferer can burn like a bushfire, scorching the soil of existence.

The accident stimulated the need for me to alter my approach to my family and friends and my directions at work. It encouraged me to change the way I had been sowing and reaping my life which had been buried deep for a decade. It began to make me understand how important it was to harvest honesty. It made me say out loud, 'I am the major hindrance to my own happiness'.

On days when I suffered these rages of unhappiness, everyone around me was awful. I would sit silently while my mind created a *Thesaurus* of invective. No one was spared: the ward staff, family, friends and especially people who had just dropped in. They could all be labelled with venom. During those hostile hours the thoughts I had about others were dark. They were so unrepresentative of what my sane feelings were that I hesitate to write about them, but I must, because those distortions were the true expressions of my state of mind at that time, and those around me had to bear their force.

Unfairly, people were regarded as cruel, unfeeling, insight-less, mean-spirited, ungenerous, vindictive, punitive, petty, poisonous, vengeful, unkind, uncharitable, calculating, small-minded, intrusive, invasive, and jealous. In most cases they were no different from the way I had always accepted them to be. What a wasteful state of mind it was. In my heart I yearned only for the return of the world of unspoilt smiles to banish the looks of awful sympathy. But my mind was merciless.

Not everyone who tried to care for me 'helped' during the moments of anger. They hardly had a chance because there is a bizarre anger in illness which shuns all kindly approaches and actively rejects them at the same time as it ferments indignation at people's neglect. What a position we put our friends and family in. They try to help and we howl for our independence. They resist their desire to assist and we scream indifference. Bizarre but believably real.

I put myself in quarantine with claims of capability. I had to learn very slowly the simple necessity of being able to say three words with genuine resignation: 'I need help'.

Someone who did help a little in the early days was one of the evening nurses. She came in each night at about half past eleven and asked if I was sleepy. If my brain was racing and I knew I wouldn't be able to sleep, she would come in to talk even though she was off duty at eleven.

There was something farm-girl about the way she wore her nurse's uniform and she told me later that she had done her training in the country. Nothing upset her. Everything was taken with natural acceptance—a real 'roll up the sleeves and get on with the job' person. She had big hands and feet. She wore brown leather row-boat shoes which she casually put up on the bedside rail, carelessly showing her open thighs without a hint of sensuous purpose. She relaxed into any position she occupied like a cozy creature and she relaxed me with her endless everyday chatter.

She was unpretentious, unaffected and one of God's children. She was free of the clutter of cleverness which stuffed my head, and she had an infallible instinct for human suffering. At least with men.

'I don't understand women,' she said. 'They always seem suspicious of my openness. But I know when a man's troubled and usually why.'

She never pushed or probed. 'I only come in here to drink your Baileys,' she said one night after I told her she was a good-hearted soul.

'You can look after yourself,' she said, knowing that was what I was trying to do in spite of needing help.

She never offered to 'help', never asked what was upsetting me and avoided all things negative. She loved to learn and always wanted to talk about the books I was reading or had read.

'Books can't teach you much mate,' I said one night after she had told me she was thinking of doing a part-time course.

'Fellas think I'm a dumb-tit sometimes,' she said. 'But it's just I say everything I think. If everyone did the same they'd look just as silly. Anyway, that's not why I want to do some study. I just want my brain to get off with itself.'

Later that night when she had gone I remembered her summary of academic pursuits as 'brains getting off with themselves' and paid for my laughter with a rib-crushing reminder.

When she left the ward I gave her a book. 'Jesus,' she said, 'I was hoping for a bottle of Baileys.'

I know in my heart we are all special, but some people have that little something extra. She was one of them. Her name was Sarah but she called herself Bill. Yet even with her I couldn't seem to manage an openness about the things which were upsetting me. But we did talk a bit about my younger life and that helped me to uncover and understand some early mysteries.

Perhaps the purely personal thoughts which came in the early hours of the morning are out of place among these specific reflections on the accident. My life did not undergo a penetrating review and awakening during the time of recovery: that came, when it arrived, in the years which followed. But there were some inner thoughts in those early weeks which involved private insights that were borne out of sleepless nights and fathered by a sorrow I can't easily explain.

One of them upset me. It was the realisation that I was rootless in terms of family heritage, and an emotional refugee. I had no sense of country, I had been born in England and brought to Australia. I had no real link to a bonded family, my mother was orphaned at five and my father lost to the family during World War II. I had no grandparents on either side, and my brother seemed to be overseas most of the time. In adult life, I had no real contact with peers because I was stuffed with self-importance and I had no close contact with everyday folk because my 'talents' encouraged me to avoid the ordinary. And I had no real desire or ability to share myself emotionally.

That sense of rootless isolation had impoverished the first half of my life and afflicted everyone of my human contacts. Now it is a little better because I have been helped to the understanding that honesty is a prerequisite for emotional growth and personal credibility is basic to any close relationship.

In the recovery ward, beset by the terrors of sleepless nights, I felt my life was wandering in a foreign territory without an emotional passport. Unable to cross borders, unable to find a way in, unable to explain where I had come from. I was bewildered by a void: the interpreters needed to translate my fragmentary version of emotional cohesion were nowhere to be found.

It is fairly fearful to be surrounded by an endless environment of feeling that you cannot meaningfully link with anyone. Now I understand I brought it on myself, unintentionally, because I had never learned how to be open about my sorrow or how to say out loud, 'this hurts inside'.

Now I am not ashamed to admit that at the time of the accident, at the age of forty-four, when the destruction and devastation of the injuries combined to produce an overwhelming emotional rubble, I missed my mother. Her own progressive mental frailty prevented her from providing me with the cradling contact of my childhood. I lay in the hospital bed hoping for some mystical earth mother to visit and nourish me. I needed someone of strength and stability whose gentleness I could trust and in whose comforts my awful inadequacies would be tolerated. None came. It was not part of ward care and my unapproachable aura of self-reliance probably prevented any approaches.

There were times when to be held close to a warm breast would have helped me more than pethidine or penicillin.

8

VULNERABLE

. . . the suffering of being

Samuel Beckett

My spirits finally came close to collapse in the hospital. I could not cope with the seemingly incessant rushes of emotional turbulence which overwhelmed me. The recurrent assaults were so severe that survival depended on each fresh incident being put to a test: will it affect whether the sun will rise tomorrow? If it didn't, I tried simply to blink it away.

Sometimes this worked. At other times I could not manage. Vague but intense apprehensions rushed towards me in crowds. Not as orderly queuing crowds, but as random rioting hordes, belligerent, destructive and oblivious of consequences. At those moments I could not tuck up my inner peril and send it to slumber. It remained awfully awake through all the early morning hours.

During the day I was aware that my appearance of passive quietness was deceptive, for while it may have been acceptable to those around me it was a symptom of profound social withdrawal and indifference. When I was an energetic doer, bossy, bristling, satirical and audacious, I was a much more caring person. That is the paradox of the social acceptability of an energy which becomes an insensibility.

At this stage of despondent quietness, I began to experience the unintentional control which silences can achieve.

Occasionally during the moments of stillness associated with this isolation I also began to appreciate the detached observations my silence allowed. But it wasn't me, and I knew it. I knew if I regained my inner abilities I would send this stranger, this still silence, packing without a wave.

I think it was Dr Johnson who said something like, 'It is easier to destroy in five minutes the human confidence built in five years'. The ease of undermining someone's confidence depends partly on the starting point of their self-esteem and partly on their inner strength at a particular moment. I was aware that in my state of internal disarray I was easier to bring down irrespective of whether my fragmentation had been caused by physical damage or the emotional assault.

Basic human regard usually encourages us to help those who are down rather than to act in a way which adds to their struggles. We do this through fundamental decency; but also because lurking in all of us is a primary feeling for our own vulnerability and our hope that, should we slip, someone passing by will give us a hand and not trample on our cliff-clinging fingers.

The memory of those who have suffered towards those who exploited their vulnerability, is as long as life itself. Some things may be forgiven but fundamental changes in one's heart demand that they can never pass from memory. Why did you do it? Why did you prey on my misfortune and exploit my weakness? Why did you kick the broken legs from beneath me?

I feel no resentment or need for retribution now. And anger only comes on those occasions when I remember how thoughtless and indifferent you were towards my suffering. I have no desire to aim for recrimination. Not because I am generous or forgiving but because I know this world has its own rough and relentless system of justice—and we all get our dues eventually.

I do not need to point my healed bones at you.

9
EARLY THOUGHTS

Ever spinning ever turning
Like the windmills of my mind

A. & M. Bergman

At this stage the days in the ward were timed by a clock which said healing can't be hurried. Thirteen weeks in plaster and that was that! At least the X-rays gave a glimpse of what was beginning to happen in the bones. What a pleasure it was to see the fine network of healing trabeculae beginning to span the breaks.

And what a sublime joy it was to have my hair washed. The running water seemed to rinse away a grimy film from my spirits. But many days came and went whose only purpose seemed to be to test my patience.

There were too many broken hours during the early weeks of recovery. They were the moments when time seemed to fracture and invite my mind to wander between its fragments.

The thoughts were intense and diffuse at the same time. My brain always seemed poised to pounce on any passing thought and turn it into a preoccupation. Sometimes I would plead for my mind to turn itself off and shut down so that I could get some peace. But back it came rolling this way and that like a restless night.

The everyday routines of life can keep lots of thoughts submerged. Sometimes that is not a good thing, but for an accident victim it has its benefits.

It is a strange phrase: 'accident victim'. If you look up the dictionary, 'accident' it explains, is: anything that happens, an event, an unforeseen contingency, a disaster, chance, fortune, an unfavourable symptom. And a 'victim' is: a living being sacrificed, someone tricked or duped, or someone injured, destroyed or damaged in any way.

I suppose I qualified as a victim but somehow I needed to cling to the belief that I was the result of how I responded to what had happened to me. I was only a victim if I responded in a victimised way. This was not just a matter of verbal delicacy. It was a real search to find an appropriate word to convey the full experience which all those involved with accidents encounter. I know 'victim' is not it because the word does not capture the personal progress which must occur if a patient is to recover comprehensively.

The blank wall opposite my hospital bed sometimes had messages on it which appeared from nowhere. One day it said 'Drive is not strength and endurance is not patience'. Alone and isolated, I had little protection against thoughts I had spent a lifetime avoiding. I knew I was hasty by nature and disinterested in much of the tiny business of life because I directed too large a proportion of my efforts into the major pursuits I tackled single-mindedly.

At the time of the accident my personal world had been consumed by physical activities which I had spent a scholastic life neglecting. In areas such as running, squash, windsurfing and swimming, I succumbed to the 'lure of the peril' and threw my body against the wind and waves without caution. I tried to explore the extreme limits of endurance with passion. They were the parts of my life I longed to be doing and which I hated to leave. Incessantly, and without any mercy, I drove myself to prove something beyond any previous achievements. The accident helped me to ask why I needed to be so relentlessly driven and so impenetrably strong.

One day late in autumn the sun shone brilliantly and the nurses were kind enough to push my bed, along with two or three others, out onto the balcony of the ward. I looked across at the open space of Royal Park with its faded grass hillocks and gums. I remembered the walks I had taken there, and the trees I'd sat beneath reading and writing, most often alone.

'Lovely to be out,' said an older man in an adjacent bed.

'Yes,' I said, 'just great.'

We sat looking out beyond the trees, revelling in the air and the light, and respecting each other's privacy. He looked extremely wasted and weak. For a long time our thoughts went their own ways.

I had always been a singular person. People were rarely permitted to enter. In the past I had always found walking alone very satisfying. There was no-one I needed either to keep up with or to catch. I could dawdle or speed at will and could stop and sit and look and laze at my own pleasure. I didn't have to consider whether others wanted to see the things I looked at. I could enjoy the delicious detail of life.

If I wanted to leap directly to a task at the top of the heap, people were not even needed as stepping stones. I rarely shared myself comprehensively with anyone and believed that no-one should ever share themselves completely. I'm not certain when I started to shed the feeling that people were mostly an encumbrance. It certainly was related to my gradual understanding that sorrow and joy both need partnership. I can only say with sadness that before the accident my life had little meaningful contact with either.

Most patients who have suffered an injury or assault ask the silent question, 'What have I done to deserve this?' I had never physically damaged anyone. I can't remember if, as a small boy, I pulled wings off insects. I don't think I did. I remember as a seven year-old hanging my teddy bear over the staircase and afterwards feeling so awful about it that I spent hours nursing him back to playfulness. I once used a broom to bop a cat which had climbed through my bedroom window and walked onto my sleeping face. And I remember accidentally striking a dog on a dark country road when taking my eldest daughter to a school camp. But none of these actions seemed to be a just source of retribution of the size I suffered. If my injuries were the expression of a relentless natural justice, then it must have been retribution for the emotional wreckage with which I had littered my life.

There were other effects and consequences following the accident which I could neither grasp nor understand. What other well-meaning people could not appreciate was that I was violently repelled by their assurances that they 'understood'.

There was also a recurring question which I struggled to answer during the early hospital weeks: 'Why did I survive?' Not, 'How did I survive such a smash?', or 'What if the car had been a metre further forwards?', or 'What if my head or spine had been shattered?' None of that. Rather it was the question, 'For what purpose did I survive?'

Having had my life threatened in a situation where no human being should expect to live, why was I spared? I wanted to feel some sense of meaning in a destiny but none came which endured the strict scrutiny of simple honesty. It wasn't to complete my tenure as a husband, father or friend, even though I had an intense sense of indignation that the accident could have ended all of them. The real reason did not reveal itself clearly. It was something mysterious which showed itself slowly and incompletely. Although my understanding of it is still limited, it involved being granted a chance to contribute to a larger harmony.

It also related to something very immediate: the indestructibility of the basic bond between my mother and me. She has been the enduring presence in my life and during the years which have followed the accident our bond has turned a full circle as I make my daily visits to her home to ensure that, in spite of her progressing Alzheimer's disease, she is in familiar surroundings, warm, clean and well fed. With her increasing need for my assistance, I feel a fundamental sense of rightness in having the chance to do for her what she had done for me single-handedly when I was a child.

During my life I have always felt safe and have been aware that my sense of security was due to her strength. I remember an occasion which occurred when I was nine years-old and which stands as the example of her strength which I cherish the most.

It happened at the Prahran Market where I was tagging along as a reluctant string bag carrier as Mum bought the week's fresh fruit and vegetables. Standing in front of a superb pyramid of oranges she requested four pounds. All went well until she noticed that the man serving her was loading the paper bag with small green blobs from the back, nothing like the orange splendour in the display. 'No,' said Mum firmly. 'I don't want those, I want ones like these.' And she simply took one from the centre of the pyramid.

I was too young to remember the war-time blitz of London, but the way the oranges collapsed was not unlike a building being bombed. They went everywhere, people kicked them, squashed them and stole them. I felt dead, certain in my nine year-old mind that we would be shouted at, punched, arrested and jailed. Not a bit of it. Mum, who was small but strong, single but strong, and foreign but strong, looked straight at the speechless stall holder and said without a trace of fear, 'That serves you right for trying to cheat me'.

I was amazed. Nothing, I thought as we walked away, can happen to me while this woman is on my side.

Once she told me the story of what happened when she went to Australia House in London in 1948 to enquire about migration. 'And what do you think you will do in Australia?' asked the somewhat imperious attendant looking down her nose at this accented single mother of two small boys who hardly knew a soul on the other side of the world.

'I shall do what needs to be done,' was her simple reply.

Another question which occupied me was what did the accident mean? In a somewhat strange sense, I could have responded to my accident and its injuries as an adventure which offered challenge, excitement and variety to the routine of my life. And in a perverse way I did. Initially, I tried to apply the same human energies and abilities to my recovery which I had used to deal with all the previous challenges in my life.

But the damage was too great, the pain too persistent and the assault on the pattern of my life too complete for me to appreciate any benefits the accident could have offered. At that time the enduring result of the whole barbaric event seemed to be a horrible memory with nothing personally ennobling. At least, nothing that could not have been achieved in a less brutal way.

I know everyone is affected differently by having their body damaged. The reclusive resent the invasion of the therapeutic army, as do the timid and shy. The gregarious battle against the restraints and the healthy, the intrusive takeovers. The homely are upset by institutional confinement and country folk by the complexity and loneliness. For me, an adventurous and restless person, the restrictions imposed by the injuries and treatment were a form of hell.

For damaged bodies, the life we come to represent can be bound by bandages and crumbling plasters, as though we had no right to claim our place. A restricted life can reduce gaiety, hard work, physical pleasure, emotional entanglements, and imagination—the best bits. Healing is simply a matter of casting aside restraints, and then accepting those which remain.

Sometimes I wonder if we should introduce some new subjects at school. For example, Acceptance; Expectations; Compulsions; Peace of Mind; and one called How Important Is It? I think exploring such subjects would help us to live our lives more sanely. It would certainly help us through the physical and emotional assaults we suffer.

On the balcony outside the ward the sun started to weaken and the air to chill. 'Not long now,' said the old man.

I knew he wasn't talking about the afternoon. 'Serious?' I asked, looking at his blood transfusion and his rapid breathing.

'They say months, but I know it's just about time. I'm ready,' he said pulling a blanket shawl over his shoulders. 'I know all this isn't going to help. I appreciate all they are trying to do but . . .' he paused, 'it's so peaceful out here.'

Later that week he died, strongly and with acceptance.

The accident forced me to make many adjustments, and my own responses helped me to accept them. I understood more clearly that human beings are shaped not so much by what has happened to them—which is often beyond their control—but rather by how they react to those events—a response which is frequently within their influence. The old man seemed to partner his own death.

In my case I had to accept that a relatively powerful body had been broken and that a sturdy spirit had been crushed. I could no longer control my speed and movement the way I had before. Things had been made imperfect through aches, pains, scars and wasting. The biggest step forwards in my recovery came when I accepted that my legs' maximum recovery would represent only a part of their previous capacity; that the ringing in my ears—my tinnitus—would not go away, and that my shoulder and ribs would continue to crunch. My responsibility was to make sure that I achieved all possible recovery.

Acceptance, adjustment and activity were the three A's of my recovery.

I learned with laser intensity that acceptance assisted recovery as much as effort. It also reduced those distortions in my mind which could cause damage to those around me. Healthy acceptance helped to prevent my distorted thoughts from turning natural human variations into profoundly unacceptable differences.

Acceptance was also a quality which tempered those moods of marauding madness during which I could stalk even those dear to me and crouch ready to leap on any human frailty and tear at it with savage intolerance. When my indignation preyed uncontrollably, it was a justified pastime for me to regard every human quality—other than those I thought I possessed—as available for attack. There is little purpose in offering a collective apology to all those who were mauled unfairly. But I do try to treat people a little better today.

10
ENERGY

I saw him once
Hop forty paces through the public street;
And having lost his breath, he spoke, and panted
That he did make defect perfection,
And, breathless, power breathe forth

After Shakespeare

By now things were healing physically. X-rays showed the callus of new bone was forming strongly and was helping to unite the bones under the plasters. My shoulder was out of its sling and was beginning to move freely and the pain in the veins of my left arm had gone.

The ribs were still crunching and it hurt to take a deep breath. For the first time in weeks I was able to sleep on my side but not on my natural right side. Each night the beat of my heart would keep me awake until the sleeping tablet numbed my brain. I was still bedfast, weak and wasted. Worst of all I had no energy. I began to understand the importance of internal strength to recovery. I knew that my loss of energy was one of my most significant injuries.

For most of my life I had been aware of an expectation on the part of those around me that I should be a reliable and responsible source of energy. As a small boy, if ever there was any trouble on the streets, I was always the one in the gang to whom the offended adults directed their sermon. And it was the same at school. In part, these expectations must have arisen quite reasonably from the person I was and the persona I projected. That I was to be the energy supplier was a conclusion probably drawn from my size, self-assurance and performance. I enjoyed those expectations and often managed to fulfill them. And while I convinced myself I had apparently unlimited human reserves, I also admitted that a nuclear reactor was required to supply the energy needed to sustain my ego. Those years were not complicated by mock modesty or humility.

Irrespective of how I view such a self-image now, at the time of the accident those perceived capacities were an essential part of my personality. I drew on them for any inspiration or leadership I was able to provide. The simple point to this is not to mock my mistaken self-importance but to explain the effects of the accident on my self-image (whatever the short-comings of that perceived image) and the subsequent effects on my sense of responsibility at home, work and elsewhere.

When my energy reserves were diverted so totally to healing, there was none left for any other endeavour. And yet all around, with my family, friends and staff, I still felt the need for me to be a reliable source of fresh energy. I therefore experienced a particularly corrosive form of self-imposed stress which was caused by my inability to maintain the support I felt was needed by others. I sensed, correctly or otherwise, their feelings of bewilderment or even betrayal. But I was as helpless to change this situation as is a drowning man who is ordered to swim. It made me feel worthless and acted against the tide of my recovery. It also produced moments of profound emotional desolation which I could share with no-one.

On occasions, that sense of void was reduced a little by the visit of someone dear. One visitor who was always a pleasure to see was my father-in-law Tom Allmand. Tom was seventy years-old and, through his life-long habits of curiosity and reading, had maintained a vigour for living and a love for learning which were lost to many men half his age. With the luxury of his retirement days, Tom was free to visit the ward during the fresh early afternoon hours.

He would arrive from his beloved Rostrum meetings each week with a parcel of love from the family in one hand, and his jovial spirits in the other. 'What reports today Tony?' he would ask.

He always directed his enquiries towards my physical progress, the medical details of which were a source of endless interest to him. I would recount the details of the respiratory function tests or the X-rays and he would follow on with a series of questions limited only by his instructions from home, 'Not to stay too long'.

Following his visits, which often resembled a medical tutorial on my part, I would turn my answers over in my mind to check that they had been both medically accurate and edited to ensure the information would not cause any unnecessary worries to the family.

Tom's visits made me aware how much we doctors take our medical knowledge for granted and how often we presume even basic medical information is known to lay people. Tom was intelligent, had an excellent general knowledge, was well read and with two medicos in the family had ready sources of clinical information. And yet his questions showed me how inappropriate and even dangerous it can be for doctors not to take the time to explain in simple language the basic details of the patient's injuries and the reasons for the choice of therapeutic options.

My injuries, a combination of multiple fractures and chest damage together with the associated circulatory and metabolic problems, were typical of many patients who suffer severe road accidents and who are spared a head injury because they were wearing a seat belt.

Fractured ribs are always intensely painful because unlike virtually all other fractures they cannot be immobilised, as the chest must continue to move during breathing. I had multiple rib fractures on both sides and an additional severe problem on the right side where the impact had caused a flail chest. This is created when a long row of ribs is broken both at the front and back of the chest. The damaged segment of chest wall does not move in the normal way—'out' when breathing in and 'in' when breathing out. Instead, it is sucked in when taking a breath and presses in on the lung and reduces, sometimes dramatically, the efficiency of drawing in air. If the segment is large enough it can render the lung on that side useless.

The pain of the fractured ribs further reduces the will to breathe deeply, and that's not all: a blow sufficiently violent to produce a flail chest always bruises the underlying lungs, and worse, as in my case, the sharp ends of the broken ribs can penetrate the lungs causing them to be punctured and collapse completely within the chest cavity—a condition called pneumothorax.

This medical mess combines these various ingredients to create a state in which air supply to the lungs and therefore oxygen to the blood and body is reduced. This situation must be corrected or the victim will die. In my case, oxygen supply and ventilation were taken over in the early days by an endotracheal tube and respirator. Had the situation gone on for longer the pressure of the tube would have jeopardised the trachea and a tracheostomy would have been done.

In all body functions, as in nature around us, everything is interconnected and related. When oxygen supply or blood perfusion is reduced every cell in the body is affected. If it is extreme you die. If it is severe the brain, which is the organ most vulnerable to lack of oxygen, will suffer. Confusion, coma or brain damage can result. If poor oxygen supply is sustained at a moderate level all healing is impaired and all wounds are vulnerable to infection. And so are the lungs, which can further reduce oxygenation and the whole vicious cycle continues.

When, as in my case, chest injuries are associated with multiple fractures in the limbs, the sequence is worsened, particularly if the fractures involve the big bones in the legs, where blood loss can be extreme but hidden as it occurs in the great muscle bulk of the thighs and calves. If uncorrected, the volume of circulating blood falls, and, together with the reduced oxygen-carrying capacity this causes, further impairs the perfusion of body tissues which can lead to surgical shock and death.

That is why major trauma victims always need rapid intravenous fluids—mine were started at the roadside—together with blood transfusions, blood pressure and cardiographic monitors and a so-called central venous pressure line, which measures the all-important clearance of blood from the lungs to the body by and via the heart. Any force great enough to break a major leg bone also severely damages the softer tissues: the skin, the underlying connective tissue and fat and the muscles. All of them bleed and so do the bones, which are rich in blood vessels. This leads to the deep bruises which appear days after the damage and gradually seep through the tissues under gravity, changing in colour from blue to purple to yellowish-brown as the blood pigment haemoglobin is broken down and absorbed. In my case the bruises across my back, loins and abdomen took two weeks to appear. Under the plasters the bruises are hidden, but frequently they show in the puffy forefoot beyond the plaster.

Every tissue in the body is affected in a patient who has a combination of multiple injuries, blood loss, impaired circulation, and the associated low blood oxygen, which is called hypoxia. It showed itself in my nails. A deep groove appeared across the nail bed from the time I was in intensive care, and took weeks to progress along my finger nails and months along my toe nails. They were like a geological band of a body-earthquake. The same thing had occurred in my hair follicles, producing a ripple wave in my hair, in my skin, in my energy reserves, and, I suppose, in my soul as well.

If the frequency of my preoccupation with the issue of energy was a true measure of its importance to healing, then it must take top place on the list of matters I thought about during my recovery. I feel these thoughts on human energy are as important as any I can share with my colleagues in health care.

During my recovery I understood that human beings had a single reservoir of energy which had three possible outlets.

The first call on one's energy is for basic survival: the energy spent on the physical, emotional and mental endeavours necessary to preserve life. Only when survival is felt to be assured is there a surplus of energy which is held in reserve ready to be used for the second call.

Secondary energy is directed into a number of tributaries which flow beyond the individual. It shows itself as the external expressions of a person's sense of self: those aspects of a life which represent the essence of an individual. Most frequently, they are the relationships which are most cherished, or the beliefs or codes in a life. Often it is a creative pursuit or hobby, and occasionally it relates to a consuming passion for a job. Invariably it is something an individual has chosen as deeply meaningful to themselves and which produces rich feelings of personal fulfillment.

Tertiary energy is the residue spent on superficial areas in which there is no real personal investment. They are not defended, they are not protected, they are not important. Our hearts are not in them. Even though we may enjoy them, we could be separated from them without consternation. In the real order of things they don't matter. We don't take them seriously and we don't care if they fade away. They could include some inappropriate people, activities, jobs and material things. Usually they are imposed on us by dubious necessity or someone else's expectations of us. If all our energies are spent in this area we have little self-esteem and even less sense of fulfillment. And we are often unhappy and unwell.

Because most of us are not engaged in a daily, demanding battle for survival an opportunity exists to direct our energy principally to the second area, towards those elements of our life which involve or flow from our inner self. They imply commitment and personal investment. We work, preserve, defend and fight for them. We are affected by them in proportion to the intensity of our involvement. Their most powerful expression could be in our feelings for those who are dear to us, our family and our friends, but often they are in our predominantly private pursuits.

I am aware of the major personal projects of my earlier life where my energy had been singularly focused and where often I had come close to achieving my goals. Each of us needed to have our own register of personal relevance because without it life could fragment into trivial pursuits.

The reason this matter concerned me so deeply was that following the accident all external expressions of my energy were amputated. None of it was used on trivia and almost nothing was left to be spent on those important activities which gave me satisfaction and which expressed what I meant to myself. All available energy was directed unvaryingly towards physical survival and emotional healing. Nothing was left. Everything else was neglected.

The inability to direct my energy to those expressions of my life which produced feelings of relevance and fulfillment left me soulless and bewildered. It felt like the spirit which was the enemy of emptiness had been taken from me.

I felt like a legless man being commanded to run.

11
EARLY RECOVERY

Nothing in nature is still,
Everything turns

The moments of early recovery will be cherished forever. All of them were private and wonderful in their simplicity.

I remember with vivid delight the first time I sat out of the hospital bed, the first time I stood up to wee, and the first blissful shower. I remember the day I managed the wheelchair to the hospital kiosk and the even more daring occasion when I went to the hospital rooftop and wept as I saw the living map of my Melbourne life all around me.

In the later months of recovery they were joined by my first buoyant, liberating swim; the happiness of transporting firewood indoors in the lap of my wheelchair; my slow, clumsy attempts at raking autumn leaves; going out on crutches to get my hair cut; and an unforgettable moment when, with a wasted wooden block of a leg just removed from plaster, I stood fixed on a squash court and smashed the black ball of my frustration sixty-eight consecutive strokes against the wall. And I didn't even care that no-one was watching. But that was months away.

The day I set out on the adventure from my ward bed to the rooftop of the hospital is still a thrill to remember. Like a freedom fighter in the underground I knew the terrain to be travelled. Twenty years earlier I had sat there in the sun reading surgical text books. Ten years before I had played table tennis in its solarium with my surgical friends.

Partnered by plasters and a wheelchair, an absconder from the confining ward room, the roof top gave me the gift of a view of my life. The old bronzed dome of Pran Central, where, thirty-two years earlier as a twelve year-old, I had nicked a wonderful music box present for Mum, from Reads, and she, knowing it was beyond my paperboy means, made me take it back. I almost got caught returning it. The southeastern suburbs where I had lived all my Melbourne life. The high school on the hill where I spent some angry, adolescent years, furious for a time at the inconvenience of being both fatherless before it was fashionable, and poor, but grateful to be bright and adventurous. The bayside beaches on which I made my first clumsy contact with girls who struggled to get their arms around me and my self-importance. The University of Melbourne where I strutted and worked to produce both dazzling displays and some distinctions. The Health Commission where I worked and where, at that time, I enjoyed the challenge of dealing with bureaucratic unmanageableness. And beyond all this, the sweep of the sea and the bay beneath the free sky. All these friends had become strangers since the smash.

I remember looking at the water for a long, longing time wondering if I would ever windsurf again and experience the silver surge of sailing into the closing sun. I thought about the time when returning from a long, slow sail across the bay I had joined some young cormorants. The board arrived in their flock silently and without causing them any fear. They rose from the water and hovered with me, not flying over or past, but simply held on the same shift of wind which drove my sail. My arms on the boom moved in harmony with the tiny tilts of the wings of a hundred birds. We were bonded in the same bank of air; each gentle fluke flowed across us in unity, we eased, hovered, hardened and moved the sail and wings with shared nonchalant precision. I was at one with the wind and the wings. It was the most perfect moment of my life—spiritual and serene.

If the accident had killed me I would have asked to come back as a sea bird, a marathon sea bird which turns the world on the wind.

As I wheeled myself back to the ward, I knew I needed to move on, slowly, silently and with better grace. Something higher had touched and guided me towards calmness.

From the sixth floor hospital window, I watched autumn transform the elms of Royal Parade. The tips turned first high in the trees and the cold stroke of winter touched the lower limbs a few weeks later. Why did they transport this magnificent European melancholy to us? Was it because all human existence is inseparable from some sorrow?

Some of the most pastel moments I experienced while in hospital occurred each week late on Friday afternoon. At that time people seemed to be surrounded by the hum of home-wardness and hurried away from the trials of their work towards the sanctuary of their homes and the weekend. Sitting beside the ward window, six storeys above the traffic, I could see people in cars and at tram stops waiting with casual tiredness and relief, glad that the toil of the week was over. Ties undone, jackets flopped over shoulders, they stood ready to catch anything which was available to carry them away from the cares of work.

I envied their freedom and opportunity. Until they were taken from me, I took for granted the importance of my end-of-week routines and social rhythms. They included the pleasure of leaving work and the relief of escaping from incessant responsibilities. They captured the need for refreshment and regeneration and the positive delights of personal pursuits and creation. The weekends provided the joy of privacy and more importantly the support and fun I shared with my family and friends. Shedding the worries and work of the week was essential to good health.

Late on Friday afternoons as a bed-fast patient—particularly when there was the added expectation and pleasure of an Australian long weekend—I always felt mellow. In hospital, restricted by plasters and platitudes, it was just more of the same. The rich rhythm of expectation was broken. The numbing repetition in the days of my long recovery drained my spirit.

It was my eldest daughter Ceri who had the keenest insight into what that confinement did to my spirits; and those spirits were always lifted when the children made spontaneous visits to the ward, often with their friends. They were quite young at that time, Ceri was fifteen, David fourteen, Tristyn thirteen and John only eleven. Whenever they came to visit I envied their freedom and their health. They had rich spirits, clear eyes, shining hair and radiant faces.

One day Tristyn arrived at the hospital with some of her friends and a scruffy looking lion toy called George. This ragged monster had been selected for me by her close friend whose nickname appropriately was Fluff. George was wonderfully ridiculous, his hair could be stroked flat and then, with a single shake it would stand up like a Rod Stewart impersonation. He sat on a shelf in the ward watching and gently warning me not to take things too seriously. It was a hard message to accept then. He still sits wide-eyed in the corner of my bedroom today, and while his message is the same it is no longer resisted.

I had to do something on the weekends so I played some games inside my head during those empty times. One of them was to make a reconstruction of an ideal life. I could select my own parents, provide everything which I felt could have been missing during my childhood and allocate every talent I wished to have. The result was quite horrible. It certainly wasn't me. Another game was to compare what I had been to what I had become. Early in my recovery that result was even more upsetting. The one game that helped a bit was to analyse why people disappointed me. The answer to that was easy. The responsibility was entirely mine: too many expectations and too little acceptance on my part.

Sometimes I filled the time with fantasies and I had a wonderful one during the last weeks in the surgical hospital. I think it was stimulated by the Olympics of that year, because I resolved to become dedicated to the goal of super fitness when I escaped from the plasters and hospital. I would eat well, exercise vigorously, sleep soundly, eliminate stress and create a significant physical challenge. It did not come to much. Being all we can be is a rather strenuous business.

Now I stroll quietly on long vagabond walks through the Peninsula Ocean Park, smelling the rhythms of nature and filled with a simple sure happiness. No marathon compulsions, no obsessive physical goals, just the steady steps of an enduring peace and an occasional long stride of the acceptance needed to cope with some people.

Some men shouldn't be doctors, especially those whose response to patients is influenced more by what they perceive a human's status to be rather than the help they need.

I suppose it was a bit naughty of me but on one occasion I made my way in the wheelchair to the hospital library and sat reading some medical journals. A consultant colleague came in and, failing to recognise me in my ward gown, produced a look of disdain at both my intrusion and presumption. My need to visit the library was a gesture, it was an attempt to try to reclaim a lost capacity and to shed my sick state.

In that hospital I had always been a doctor and my library visit was a way of trying to restore my medical confidence. My colleague's look put me in my patient's place and confirmed his limitations.

I knew I was getting stronger when I didn't become angry but just shrugged his silliness away. And there were other examples of that returning strength.

In the ward, at first I was impotent to act against the disregard I occasionally saw expressed by staff towards patients who had neither the will nor the skill to fight for themselves. It was upsetting to realise I could be brought to a state where I had lost the capacity to act on my justified indignation. But the recovery of my will to speak up and say, 'That behaviour is unacceptable,' was a welcome return of my inner strength.

My most dramatic encounter with wilful carelessness happened this way. I was sitting in my wheelchair waiting for the ward lift. When its doors opened a nurse began walking out backwards as she guided an empty bed over the floor gap. The bed was being pushed by a hospital orderly whose speed of exit meant that I would need to get out of the way very quickly. But wheelchairs don't move sideways. The wall was behind me and the nurse and the bed were rushing towards my outstretched plastered legs. 'Hey stop!' I shouted in real panic.

Instinctively the nurse slowed the bed against the continuing thrust of the orderly. She was as distressed as I was furious. 'What are you doing?' she said to him with alarm.

My expectations of caution from the orderly were as misplaced as my anticipation of an apology. 'You shouldn't sit there Tiger,' he called nonchalantly over his shoulder as he trolleyed the bed away. 'You're likely to be flattened mate.'

Three or four lifts came and went as I sat congealed with

disbelief and anger. My God, I thought, if he treats reasonably substantial humans like that, how does he handle those who are frail, elderly or unable to speak English.

Two weeks passed before I encountered him again. This time I was in the lift and he was waiting with a dozen people outside in the foyer. I rolled my wheelchair into the light beam of the lift door bringing everything to a momentary halt, then looked straight at him and said with deliberate intensity. 'The other week you almost rammed a bed over my broken legs. You are irresponsible, careless and discourteous at best, and a bloody stupid menace at worst. You ought to be sacked. And just for the record the name is not Mate or Tiger but Dr Tony Moore.'

I'd had two weeks to organise what I wanted to say but in view of the surrounding staff I spared him the worst. I gained some satisfaction in setting the matter straight, but my good thoughts about having regained enough energy to take a forceful stand on my own behalf were short-lived. The next day up to my bedside came the union representative of the would-be tiger tamer asking me to consider an apology for 'Having humiliated one of the members publicly'. He had been 'Very upset, almost in tears,' I was told.

I asked the union representative had he had the chance to speak with the nurse who had prevented our tearful terror from crushing my legs. 'No,' he said. 'Different union.'

I told him very nicely to piss off.

By now, I was quite mobile in my wheelchair and was waiting for the final week of my three months in the Royal Melbourne Hospital when they planned to take one plaster off completely and change the other from full-leg length to one below my knee. I also needed to have some screws removed from my right ankle. I was looking forward to the procedures because they meant I was one step closer to going home and starting at the rehabilitation hospital. But I nearly brought the whole thing undone by carelessness.

Wheelchairs are acceptable if you know they are temporary. As a step forwards in recovery they produce the same sort of thrill as getting a drivers licence—and for the same reasons. They offer mobility, independence, speed and freedom; but like cars they can be very dangerous if handled carelessly. In spite of advice and knowledge, I leant forwards to push a hospital lift button and went down like an over-eager child on a playground slide, landing flat splat on my back.

Beached whales usually die and I know why. They die of humiliation. If you plan to tip your wheelchair over do it when there are a few people around, preferably weight lifters, or you will spend quite some chastened time on the floor. And don't do it on the day before you are due to be discharged or you might finish up where you started.

It was not from any sense of ingratitude that I threw all the 'Get Well' cards and letters into the bin when I finally left the ward. I tried to reply to them all even though, at the time, my handwriting resembled a wavering and ominous electrocardiograph.

The cards were like autumn leaves: it was their destiny to fulfill their worth then fall. I wanted to move on to the springtime of my recovery and desiccated leaves had no place there. They had supported me through a season of survival by transporting the warmth of kindness. The only ones I kept were the letters from the children. They were filled with the magic of rainbow rain.

Someone once said, 'Whenever we do anything for the last time, provided we have done it regularly before, we are a little melancholy even though it has been distasteful to us'.

I suffered not one mite of melancholy when I was finally freed from the hospital.

12
OUTSIDE

It is good to be out on the road,
And going one knows not where

John Masefield

The first warning that I would need to make some changes
in the way I tackled tasks came one minute after I had passed
through the hospital doors. In a heedless hurry I tried to slide
from the wheelchair to the car seat without supporting my
left leg. Fresh out of its long plaster its thigh was wasted to
the bone and provided no strength to support the plaster below
my knee. The weight of the cast dropped to the pavement
and tore at the ligaments in my knee which hadn't moved
for ten weeks and ripped at the muscles in my thigh. The
joy of leaving the hospital lasted only as long as my impulsiveness.
It was the beginning of an enduring apprenticeship in which
I had to adapt to both new limitations and feelings of physical
vulnerability and exposure.

Only those who have spent months of enforced bed-rest
can appreciate how rough are our roads. The first car trip
from the surgical hospital to the rehabilitation centre was
alarming. I was driven in a car which, while ageing gracefully,
was quite smooth on the road. But every corrugation, every
dimple and ripple on the road, shook me silly. I kept pleading,
'Slow down'. When you haven't moved at even walking pace
for months, a car seems to roll along at Formula 1 speed even
if the driver is cautious.

In the following weeks during my daily visits to the rehabilitation hospital, I was subjected to the appalling driving antics of many taxi drivers. They sped, they swerved, they stopped suddenly and, somewhat surprisingly, they took very unkindly to even mild suggestions that they were unfit to drive dodgem cars.

In the streets the light was bright, things moved very quickly and sounds were loud. The city world was so unstill. The air was cold and full of fumes. People's faces were blank, worried or angry. Smiles were rare and tenderness hurried past without any pause.

I wanted to hide in the private seclusion of home.

13
HOME

He that outlives this day and comes safe home

Shakespeare

Coming home was a happy event. The children had put up a banner across the drive welcoming me back. The house was so beautifully quiet compared with the ward room—which had the misfortune to be near the pan disposal area and its cymbal crashing sounds—and there was the luxury of my own bed and bathroom. What a delicious treat returning to my own bed after three months of fragmented sleep.

The peace and quiet made it easier to sleep, but the more deeply I slept the more difficult it was to stretch out the stiffness the next day. As soon as I moved in the morning I knew what the day would bring. Sometimes it was easy, other days it was not worth going on. In winter the tiredness and pain made it a calvary to twist out of bed and shoulder another day's burden. But the consequences of not making it to the rehabilitation hospital for treatment were far worse than the work of getting up. Any surrender wrecked the chance of recovery.

The winter mornings glued my joints. Everything had to be eased awake ever so carefully because if I tried to enjoy a long luxurious yawn-like stretch, the major leg muscles would seize into spasm. When this happened they could be coaxed out of their cramps only with the help of a near-boiling bath.

The morning bath was one of the reliable times of the day. Like everyone recovering from multiple fractures, I always felt a sense of bliss in its warmth. My body was also relieved of the burden of bearing its own weight by the buoyancy of the water. It was the closest thing to returning to the safe, silent warmth of the womb—something even grown men occasionally wish to do when they feel helplessly dependent.

For differing reasons, the early morning and the late evening were the worst times of the recovery day. Dawn was difficult because of the effort needed to unlock the body from its sense of emptiness and inertia. Twilight was a trial because at the end of the day a tired brain, physical fatigue and a weary spirit combined in a conspiracy as I struggled to cope with the enduring significance of the injuries. During the day, business buffered the mess somewhat. On bad days the conspiracy got through and stabbed me.

It was the incessant nature of the injuries which was the source of such sharp torture. The injuries were with me each day, at all times, everywhere. They were like wild animals which watched and tracked me home with malevolent curiosity. The more I angrily threw stones at them the more they snarled with goading satisfaction. I felt like screaming, 'Go away, leave me in peace!' Sometimes the shout came and people thought it really was directed at them. But my anger gradually faded, along with my memory of what it was like to have an intact body.

If the pain didn't get through, the cold did. One day in early winter, I sat in my wheelchair at the front gate waiting for my younger son to come home from school. You can't jiggle and shuffle yourself warm in a wheelchair. Your body provides an easy, static target for the cruel antarctic winds. And when it has lost lots of flesh it has little protection against the teeth of winter. John was dawdling his way home and I began to feel ill in the cold. I came inside, crawled into a warmed bed and shivered and went on shivering for several hours. I could not regain my internal warmth. Mawson must have been a god to survive his journey.

When I first tried to get up on crutches for a short moment it felt like a mid-winter Monday morning. It just hurt. The aches affected every joint. If I had been wise I would have avoided having a recovery in mid-winter. Cold gets into broken bones so easily and the more bones you have broken the more likely it will be to chill the marrow of your mind as well.

I had to keep busy to deflect my anger and sorrow. Even for a free spirit the routines and rituals of life are reassuring. I remember in my compulsive academic days the joy of simply shopping or washing a car when the exams were over. Everyday activities were enjoyed because they were free of the toil of heroic achievement. It was the same at home in a wheelchair. I could try small tasks and even though I was clumsy and slow I loved doing them. As the season had just touched winter I spent many moments raking garden leaves into small mushy mounds. It must have looked very silly from the street. Wheelchairs are so hard to push on soft grass and using the rake made me feel I was in a boat paddling imperfectly in a soggy pond of mulch. By mid-afternoon, when the sun slipped away and the clean, cold of June touched the trees, I left the rake in the care of the liquid amber and busied myself with the firelogs. Wood on wheels at three pm.

Never have I enjoyed the friendliness of an open fire so much as during that winter. Fires converse with people who are alone. They touch all the senses: their twisting ribbons of light, their sounds and smells, and the touch of their enduring warmth. I sat fixed in front of the glowing flames, free of the desire to debate or discuss or do anything. It was the most splendid sort of rest I had during the whole period of recovery. Open fires—something else which is not mentioned in today's medical texts.

The moments in front of its flames were sometimes shared by the children when they came home from school. After their kitchen raid they would come and say hello. But they were still unsure of how to help an injured father. I wished that the trust and endearment felt between me and my children was a matter of direct feeling rather than the simple fact of me being their father. There is more chance of that being the case now than before the accident. There was no chance of it at all while my moods were unhinged by the strain of recovery.

At home my tiredness and pain created problems. I had restricted mobility and strength; and from the confinement of my wheelchair I saw things which needed to be done around the house but which I couldn't manage. The children, behaving with perfect adolescent indifference, walked past jobs in the house and garden without either a blink of concern or the slightest concession to my compulsion for tidiness. I tried so hard not to say anything, each day, worse at night, worse as the week wore on, until on Sunday eve, after they had had the whole weekend to themselves, noticing nothing, doing little, I couldn't restrain myself from asking them to help. Then they reacted as if I had committed a crime. I can only say I was worse when I was their age. And anyway it is a 'father's job' to be home-help and handyman. But it hurt. Sometimes I felt what I imagined to be their unspoken indignation that I had it easy, resting in bed, reading and not doing anything about the house.

Before the accident I struggled to find a way to contribute the things I had to offer the children and that filled me with sadness. The accident made me realise that the problem was as much a matter of my style as my substance. I was too intrusive and too critical of their interests and I needed to be more supportive of their ways. Rather than get angry at the time they spent with television, I began to ease into their programmes and the conversations they created. I stopped regarding television as visual valium and accepted it as something that I could share with them. The fact that it was not 'ideal' was irrelevant—it was better than isolation. Those concessions began a process of creative surrender for me.

In the time before the accident, being a father was occasionally like being on a diet—an enduring trial which was difficult to sustain. I had always struggled to engage in small talk; and as most conversation in a family is everyday chatter, it was not easy for me to reach a natural conversational rhythm with my children. I am sure that they were hesitant to ask me questions for fear the answer would turn into a major oration. I had always been more interested in talking about 'major' matters, or myself—neither of which assists good talk with kids. I must have appeared busy, lofty and disinterested in their world. And as we went about our separate business I was not confronted by the great shortcomings of my communication with them. On holidays however, or in hospital, or at home convalescing, with inescapable contact, I could not hide my inadequacies.

The unfortunate thing about my fatherhood was that

although I wasn't always around I was always in the way. At the time I returned home my inner disharmony and anger were so great the children understandably gave me a wide berth. I couldn't control the chaos of my inner life and its aggressive turbulence surfaced and swirled in my warlike responses to my wife and family. 'I'm going and that's that,' I said with the beginning of a tremble at the edge of my voice.

'But you are still dizzy when you stand up,' pleaded the family.

'Not if I move slowly,' I argued with wild force and little conviction.

'Then we will use the wheelchair,' said my wife.

'I shall *walk* from the car on my crutches,' I insisted, refusing to concede. 'It's only twenty metres from the car park to the bench, and I can sit there for the whole school sports, or, if we find out when John's 400 metre event is on we can make a quick round trip.'

They looked at each other, then to the sky, and were silent. It happened at a time in my recovery when I felt my spirit was slipping away. I needed to associate myself with positive, courageous and successful things; and my son John's swift victories in athletic events—like my son David's soccer goal-scoring skills—were a guaranteed source of delight. John still holds two or three school records almost a decade later, and I wanted to be there to support him and to return a tiny bit of the massive support and love he was providing for me at home. And I wanted to stand up in front of the school parental herd and with my presence silently shout, 'My children still have a living father'.

Getting into the car was a slow but successful process and the steady trip to the school oval passed comfortably. Then the silliness started as I shunned my wife's offers of assistance. I stood up in a tracksuit, a symbolic costume but sadly one which was as synthetic and superficial as my own posturing physical strength, then struggled forwards unsteadily, not stopping at the first easy bench but going on with a stare fixed to the uneven ground just in front of the scaffold of crutches which wobbled me forwards. Groups of parents were passed and my wake brought a wash of sympathetic whispers which drove me on like a man possessed. Then, just as I was into a more confident rhythm, one of the fathers who had a courtroom boom in his voice, exclaimed incredulously, 'That's not Tony Moore!'

I had to stop at the next bench. I suppose he was right. Almost unrecognisably wasted, and without the radiant energy which was his mark, he really wasn't Tony Moore.

John won by the length of the straight and I stood up. A victorious tendon-slim and swift eleven year-old embraced his foolish forty-four year-old father with a hug which said, 'Dad, we both know why we are here, even if the others don't'.

The walk back to the car was unmanageably long, hard and full of hurt. I was grateful to get home.

Gradually, during my convalescence, the periods of self-reflection in front of the fire allowed me to gain some personal insights which improved my approach to being a better father. All of these helped to prevent me from being a persistent barrier between our mutual affections. I realised that my children had a primary right to their own space and emotional air, that they had a right to be happy or unhappy in their own way, and the right to make their own successes or mistakes in their own way.

It wasn't all growl and grumpiness. On one occasion when I tried to do too much in the garden my thigh muscles went into spasm—muscles which create ten times more pain than cramps of the calf. I was rolling around on the lawn in agony trying to unlock the spasm. I must have looked quite a sight thrashing about on the grass. But the pain dissolved into laughter when one of the children quipped, 'Wouldn't a lawn mower be easier?'

On that occasion I didn't go into a silent emotional binge because I hadn't received the sympathy I thought was 'due' to me.

Being busy with everyday household tasks was not the only activity which helped prevent a recovery day from moving in the wrong direction. Small achievable goals assisted too. It was important during each day of my restoration to feel that something had been accomplished, no matter how insignificant. I tried hard to practise the discipline of setting at least one tiny task I knew could be managed. Sometimes, it was a page to be read, occasionally it was a few paragraphs to be written, often it was a simple job around the house, or speaking to a friend on the phone. On those difficult days when everything seemed to be an overwhelming effort, quietly listening to special music was an achievement. Those tiny triumphs, especially my reclaimed physical capacities, provided the first real building blocks of my body's recovery.

One challenge which gave me great pleasure was archery. It was an activity I started at the rehabilitation hospital and continued at home in the afternoon. I set up the straw target in front of an old mattress leaning against the garage wall and rolled the wheelchair back up the drive, stood for a few seconds and let the arrows fly. Besides strengthening my shoulder and arm and improving the fine control of my fingers it released frustration. It was truly remarkable the sources of anger whose image appeared in the bull's-eye. Provided I did not stay out too long I got sharper and sharper.

Peter De Grant used to join me when he came to visit. Always endeared to simple pleasures he would try hard but would never let me lose.

He was so peaceful and so accepting—an unusual combination in a doctor. It was always a joy to see his scruffy old duco-bare Volkswagen chug up the street. 'No I don't ever wash the car,' he said. 'It doesn't expect me to. It's an agreement between us. I'm not expected to wash it and it doesn't expect to wash me.'

We would come inside and sit beside the fire and talk. 'I would have stopped,' he said.

'Stopped?'

'Yes, I don't think I could have found the power to do what you've done so far.'

'Sometimes I feel I'm trying too hard.'

'You could do it easier by concentrating on the broken bits.'

'How?'

'Picture your leg in your mind,' he said. 'Concentrate on the muscle groups under the plaster and put them into static contraction. You don't have to move the joint to contract it.'

'I'll try,' I said, and I did, and it worked.

He always left me with something valuable. 'Time is never wasted, even when it's wasted,' he said one day as he disappeared on seeing another visitor about to arrive.

Through his easy company and fine insight, Peter lifted my spirits.

It was after one of his visits that I took a big social step and went to see the film *Amadeus*. It was a mistake. The seats were too uncomfortable, the film was too long, pain relief was unavailable and the inappropriate American accents! It was quite some time before I went out again.

When I did it was quite enjoyable. And it is a small world. During the wheelchair phase of my recovery I went to see Torvill and Dean skate. The care and consideration given to those in the audience who were wheelchair-bound was exceptional, to such a degree that I wrote a letter of appreciation to the management.

They must have been pleased because they sent a copy of the letter to the Health Department as a mark of what they had achieved for disabled people. The Minister for Health, in turn, sent it down to the head of the department responsible for services for aged and disabled people—who was me.

So my own letter arrived on my own work desk many months later! Fortunately, the Minister had not asked me to draft a reply. Talking to yourself is one thing, but writing official replies . . .!

14
REHABILITATION

*Oh spare me a little, that I may recover my strength
before I go hence, and be no more seen.*

Book of Common Prayer

My first moments in the rehabilitation hospital were upsetting.
Even though I was a doctor and had visited the hospital two
or three times before, and in spite of knowing what it did
and how it worked, it was one of the most emotionally distressing
days of my recovery.

I sat in a wheelchair in the corridor feeling abandoned
and lost, emotions which were made worse by the sight of
more severely injured co-patients. Those with major injuries,
particularly brain damage, affected me deeply.

I knew some were capable of only moderate improvement
and were facing a future of long-term deficits with all the undermining consequences for their job and their joys. Looking into
their faces I sensed they knew it too. One could touch the
anxiety and anger which surrounded them. Worse than that
was the mute, defeated, helpless resignation which afflicted
those who had surrendered, or who had been overwhelmed
by their damage.

At first I was glad I was to be there only as a day patient
and to be at home for the rest of the time. But quite quickly
I appreciated that without the skills of the rehabilitation team
my physical recovery and those of my co-patients would have
been delayed many months.

The challenge of moving in the morning was met partly by fear. If you succumb to inertia you sink. If you stay in bed late, if you don't shave, if you don't pick up the rhythm of the day and get to the hospital you will slip slowly down. Some mornings it felt impossible. Fortunately all mornings were improved by a long hot bath and a cup of strong coffee. It was the same when I arrived at the rehabilitation hospital. Some days the body begged for respite and the mind could not muster any further motivation. The weights in the gymnasium seemed twice as heavy and it felt as though the brakes had stuck on the exercise bike. Even dressing was an ache-ridden ordeal.

The problem was that those feelings of wretchedness were always made worse by a failure to meet the challenge of the day. On those damnable days, I went to a spa in the afternoon. The warm liquid weightlessness was just splendid; and the sense of sensuous flow across my naked skin helped me to forget the pain.

The Hampton Rehabilitation Hospital staff led by Dr Denis Kininmonth did a perfect job on my physical recovery. I progressed with my strength and mobility at a great rate. And it was fun being there. But lurking beneath every physical improvement was a swamp of unresolved emotional pain which I had still not been courageous enough to reveal to anyone. In fact, I used my preoccupation with physical progress as a bridge to span the psychological swamp; and it worked for a long time.

The physiotherapy and hydrotherapy helped to tune the roughened structure of my body. The perception expressed in the physiotherapist's hands was superb as they moved my joints to the limits of their rusty range without causing me any pain. Even the physiotherapy students whose touch was tentative helped me on my journey. And the occupational therapists, whose skills I believed I knew, were of considerable help to me with both personal recovery and a true understanding of their talents. Everything they encouraged me to do was specially selected to alleviate my specific problems. The rug I weaved and the wood I sanded helped the strength and range of movement in my shoulder. The baskets whose bases I drilled improved them further and through its foot-pedal drive assisted the strength of my floppy ankles.

Best of all was the skittle set I invented and fashioned on the lathe. Its production was a boost to both my hand coordination and my spirits. It was an ingenious project because each tiny skittle was self-standing through a pull string which went through its barrel and then under the rolling board to the front. Pulling the ten strings sprung them to attention. Beautiful chrome ball bearings were used as bowls and the children loved playing with it. Making it took me back to my days at Prahran Technical School in the fifties where woodwork was a favourite subject.

My rehabilitation had more to do with musculoskeletal re-education than healing. It was such a positive environment because patients relearned how to balance, transfer, walk and be active. They got better by improving functions on which the pleasures of life depended. But the patients had to do all they could to help themselves otherwise the therapist was battling to improve them. And occasionally it could bring the most unexpected improvements.

Sexual surges came as improbable carnivals during recovery. Plastered limbs are a clumsy prophylactic. One occurred as I lay dutifully on the physiotherapist's couch when a long-legged occupational therapist in a cotton dress wandered through a wonderfully penetrating beam of springtime sunshine to ask me if I was happy with my progress. 'Yep,' I replied emphatically.

The most pleasant of all my rehabilitation hospital experiences were the blissful moments I spent in the warm surrounds of the hydrotherapy pool. Hydrotherapy is not just fun and games in the water, even though there can be lots of bubbly joy in the pool. It is a highly skilled form of physiotherapy which uses the properties of water in a therapeutically purposeful way. On the one hand, the buoyancy of the water relieved everyone in the pool who had leg weakness or wasting of the burden of supporting their body weight. This provided a beautiful feeling of liberation enabling the return of some of the functions our injuries had taken from us. On the other hand the resistance of water—over three hundred times that of air—encouraged significant muscular effort when any part of our bodies was moved against its density, as anyone who has tried to run in the shallows of the beach knows. And its heat! Just below body temperature, it welcomed you into its warmth. For the first few moments I clasped the sides of the pool with my arms fully stretched, and let the warmth and weight of the water float me effortlessly. It was like experiencing a blend of a total embrace and a gentle massage.

Then the work began. Slow, easy stretches to free up the glue in grating joints, then repeated muscle contractions, varying in force and focus and finishing with a game designed to compliment the objectives of the strengthening programme. One game was water volleyball, where useless legs could be partially compensated by the support of the water, and where players could achieve moderate leaps that felt Olympian to a recovering mind. Clumsy and uncoordinated, we all tried to win for our team and ourselves. The point at which sporting ingenuity became flexibility in the interpretation of the 'rules' or even fun-filled cheating was not important. Some of us almost drowned in gulping waves of laughter.

I watched the courage and confidence of the younger patients grow in the pool. They could see discos and driving and just happy drifting as real possibilities after a good session of hydrotherapy. Stiffness dissolved, pain was reduced and things which were impossible only an hour earlier were achieved. It showed in their faces. It was the radiance of reclaimed possibilities. It was often a shared sensation and produced the strong, silent comradeship of real progress.

Not everyone there was committed to their own wellbeing. One of my rehabilitation co-patients was a cadger. She was a mine of information on every lurk and perk injury could offer. Day after day I could hear the ceaseless hum of her mosquito mind and the buzzing of her voice advising anyone who would care to listen on the best way to live off the system. She had decided what would be the most rewarding limits to her recovery and that was that. Compensation preoccupation is worse than prostitution. In selling a part of one's body the whole self is sold short.

As patients we all needed to feel that our progress towards physical recovery was sustained. That was why each of us secretly celebrated even a tiny gain. That was why any setback, delay or complication could sometimes be a source of devastation. That was why shedding restrictions such as plasters, braces, wheelchairs, crutches and assistance brought such joy, and their retention such distress.

I remember one occasion when I was waiting anxiously for a review X-ray of my leg and I started to sweat at the prospect of films which might show that the fracture had failed to unite. This was the final X-ray, and its result was the only thing which could go wrong with what had been the unhindered progress of my physical injuries. The man beside me in the X-ray waiting booth, whose plaster suggested he had also broken a tibia, asked me if I was feeling all right. 'Yes. Just a bit tense about the X-ray result.'

'I know the feeling,' he said. 'Mine's gone the wrong way. They're talking bone graft now. It's over six months and it still hasn't knit.'

'Have they explained the problem to you?' I asked.

'Not really. Just said some do—some don't, the luck of the draw I suppose. The worst thing is I've tried to do everything right. Followed all the instructions.'

'It's that particular bone,' I said wondering if his non-union was an omen for me.

'You something medical?' he asked, looking at my glasses.

'Yes.'

'No-one is spared, eh?'

'Nope.'

'Well at least you know what's going on.'

'Yes,' I said. 'And what can go wrong, and right now that's making things worse.'

'Your's going all right?'

'So far,' I replied. 'But today is the important one. If the healing looks good it will be out of trouble.'

'Why is this bone such a difficult fella?' he asked, lowering his voice a little as if to invite me into a medically conspiratorial discussion.

'You're right.' I said. 'The big shin bone, the tibia, has a bad reputation. Often the fracture is caused by a twist and it can produce a spiral fracture or a free fragment of bone which doesn't unite well. It's usually possible, with careful orthopaedic management, to pull it back into alignment and hold it there with a plaster or a metal plate. But the actual healing of the bone can be slow because of the blood supply.'

'What do you mean?'

'Well, most bones get their blood supply from both ends, so when it's fractured, both edges have enough arteries to provide nutrition to help the new bone form. But the tibia gets its blood from the upper end almost exclusively. Very little comes through the lower fragment of bone which can then struggle to heal.'

'Is that what's happened to mine?'

'You'd have to ask your surgeon. But it's likely to be the reason, particularly if there was no infection of the leg or gross fragmentation of the bone. It's called non-union.'

'And there's nothing I can do about it?'

'Nothing you haven't done if you've followed the surgeon's instructions. There are general things which help healing, like good nutrition, good circulation, adequate rest and good general health, but you look fit and well fed.'

He patted his stomach. 'A bit too much of the amber diet there,' he said.

'If you eat well and drink in moderation that shouldn't directly affect the fracture healing.'

'And why a bone graft?'

'Usually when the fractures in this bone fail to unite the surgeons do an operation to freshen up the bone ends to help them stick together and then pack around the fracture with bone chips taken from the hip bone, which, when they take, add a sort of bone cement to the area.'

'If it's got to be done then so be it. But I'm sick of the whole thing. It's hard to get on with it when they say, "Don't put any weight on the leg," and "The plaster has got to stay on".'

'I know mate,' I said.

I was often prepared to pay with discomfort for the prospect of pushing my body to limits already crossed by my mind. There were many times when my recovery ran forwards faster in my mind than in my limbs. While they were moments of frustration at least it was a vigorous disappointment. Less frequent, but more upsetting, were the occasions when my emotions lagged behind my legs.

At one stage my plaster became my foe. It had never felt comfortable, pressing on the front of my left shin. It was also an imperfect, ugly, lumpy job which had grown loose with muscle wasting. Claiming that the pain under the plaster was worse than it was—bad pain is always reason to consider changing the plaster—I returned to the outpatients department at the Royal Melbourne Hospital. I had not been there since my discharge and the sight of the building with the window on the sixth floor made me feel ill.

I went straight to the plaster technician. Ken was a master craftsman. The way he fashioned the new cast made it feel like it was a natural companion to the healing bones. It looked clean and beautifully finished with all the edges smoothed to save the skin from friction. This skilled sculptor must have gained his satisfaction from the job for he received pathetic pay, simply because there was no award or position for a plaster technician at that time. I left the plaster room feeling refreshed and without knowing why, called in to the intensive care ward. The staff who remembered me were overjoyed with my progress. 'Not many come back,' said one of the nurses somewhat ambiguously.

The nurses expressed a real delight at seeing my state of recovery. I thanked them with a hug and was moved by their delight at my progress. One said, 'I didn't realise you were so tall'. For someone who could have lost his legs, it was a good thing to hear.

Another asked, 'No bad memories of ICU?'

'No,' I admitted truthfully. 'But I see the radio is still pounding.'

'Yes,' she said. 'Some people believe it stops the night-mares about ICU after they get out.'

'Patients or staff?' I asked.

Personally, I had only one truly terrifying dream during the whole ordeal. It occurred towards the end of my formal rehabilitation about seven months after the accident. I dreamt I was drowning at the bottom of the hydrotherapy pool and no-one would come to save me. The silly thing is that the pool is a bit like life: you only have to stand up to realise it's really not deep enough to drown in. It's up to you.

Some healthy people regard disabled people as lepers. At one stage I overcompensated intentionally to create an impression of health beyond the reality. I lost weight, went to the gymnasium to do extra sessions to strengthen the improving bits of my body, and got a springtime tan. All this was done to avoid questions, sympathy and the stain of sickness.

I remember with vivid delight when the limp finally left,

and I could walk evenly down the street with no obvious sign of injury. Provided I did not hurry, the stiffness and cramps could be kept to myself. But occasionally, when I had to move quickly to avoid a pram, a hurrying pedestrian or, more fearfully, a car, I would respond instinctively and forget the limitations in my legs. Then I would wince and stop and curse.

On one occasion I had an embarrassing disaster. I had gone to Southland shopping centre on crutches to feel the normal rhythm of browsing in shops. Standing in front of a clothing store minding my own business I was mortified to see a happy five year-old running her own pusher towards me at big dipper speed. I tried to protect myself, stumbled, grabbed hold of the rack of clothes outside the shop and went down in an anxious flurry of limbs, crutches, child, pusher and clothes. I sat in the middle of the display draped in a floral dress which really did nothing for me.

Many patients who break a leg or smash a knee take for granted the ease of using crutches. But it isn't that simple. Wholesome hospital instructions which help patients to use them in a commonsense way do not capture the essence or Zen of crutches. Humans have taken two hundred thousand years to evolve efficient walking, and everything about that progress has been directed towards mechanical efficiency and the conservation of energy. We still have the mechanical musculoskeletal structure of hunters and gatherers.

I once remember seeing a graphic display of a man walking with a light fixed to his centre of gravity. The plot of the light moved in an almost effortless, gentle undulation: a broad sweeping sine wave of the lowest amplitude. The reason was simple: to minimise the work of lifting the body against gravity, and to reduce the energy needed to prevent it plunging into the ground under the influence of gravity. The powerful muscles on the front of our thighs and shins have not been designed just to allow us to kick or jump, but to act against gravity when we walk or run. Our most energy-efficient movements are skating on ice, rollers, or a board, because on a level surface there is no expense of energy against gravity. Running and especially jumping are the most gravity-confronting activities. We really do glide when we walk; a foot drop of only one half-centimetre can cause the front of our shoe to catch any unevenness in the walk surface. And we are designed to walk all day with energy-conserving efficiency provided all our leg muscles and joints are in harmonious working order. But add a limp or an imbalance, or, worst of all, crutches, and we rapidly find out how inefficient those abnormal gaits are.

Using crutches is always tiring, but using them after major damage has imposed months of bedrest and wasting is totally exhausting. These crutches, which were designed to help us, can also become a hindrance. They immobilise our hands and arms; they cause dangerous balance problems if one tries to carry anything on them—back packs are essential—and they can cause havoc in the shoulders as the weight of one's body is carried abnormally by these joints.

But it does not pay you to declare war on them as I did. I struck their rubber tips into submission on pavements and pathways with all the force of my frustration. And their worn metal-bare ends retaliated by slipping on a concrete surface sending me spinning like a one-legged heron trying to high jump. Even when I agreed to call a truce and began to treat them gently they didn't forget my earlier aggression. They punished me with shoulder pain. Supraspinatus tendonitis it was called: a condition in which the tendon of the small muscle which helped to lift the arm from my side was crushed into excruciating inflammation beneath the arch of the collar bone. The pain was so bad I could not reach across to lift the passenger car door button when taking the children to school. I never really made friends with my crutches and hurried off them as soon as it was safe.

On the weekends I drove my Moke. No problems with door knobs—no doors. There is something very cheeky about a Mini Moke and there was something very naughty about a person with a leg in plaster driving one after an accident.

Some sorts of irresponsibility are essential to recovery, especially when they help produce an emphatic, liberating 'so there' thump on the chest. I indulged my irresponsibility on a few occasions. I tried to run around the Albert Park Lake the day after a plaster was removed. The leg was like a block of wood, there was no elastic give and little muscle power to buffer the impact. The shock waves went up the leg and thigh and through the pelvis to the muscles at the side of my abdomen. After thirty metres I limped lamely back to the car with an 'Oh well', which is recovery's reverse side of 'So there'.

Driving the Moke was a better form of creative irresponsibility. It was so liberating to leave behind the humiliation of waiting for someone to drive me, and to be subjected to their version of traffic terror The top of the plaster just made it under the steering column. All Mokes have a sense of humour, that's why people smile at their drivers. And the look of the thing, sent unfinished into the world, no windows, no warmth, just the delicious reviving wash of the wind. They were happy moments of wilful independence.

I reached a stage where I knew I had to do everything within my abilities to make sure I didn't tire of the physical goals. There were five matters which needed attention:

> Instinctively, I tried to eat well: no sugar, no processed food, and a return to eating food which was as close to its natural state as possible.

> I wanted to exercise one or two hours a day: cycling was the only aerobic exercise I could manage but the indoor exercise bike was simply ridiculous. So I walked on my crutches.

> It was easy to take the step of eliminating all foreign substances including analgesics, sleeping tablets, coffee and saccharin. I got rid of all of them.

> It was not so easy to ensure I managed good long sleep—because of the cramps, tinnitus and pain.

> I learnt to walk away from incidental undermining stresses, or smiled them down saying, 'I understand but I cannot become involved'.

The gymnasium was a help for awhile. I joined soon after I left the rehabilitation hospital, spending the first half of the afternoon trying to regain further strength. But I soon encountered a problem: the fitter I became in terms of muscle development, the more I was confronted by the limitations imposed by my injured joints. My body became stronger but the damage to my ankles and shoulder limited what I could do with that fitness. It simply became another form of reduction and another symbol of loss. It produced a trough in which the most dangerous phrase to be heard in recovery began to echo: 'Why bother'.

One strategy which often helped to shift horrible feelings was a visit to the hairdresser. It seems a fairly everyday thing to get a haircut, but the ritual of libation, the feel of cleansing warm water and the gentle caress of fingers through my hair were wonderful.

My regular hairdresser was a real character. 'Where do you want me to put your crutch?' she asked with intentional ambiguity as I flopped into the chair.

'I don't think it would make very good kindling at the moment,' I said somewhat feebly.

'Well sit down Doc and help me with my problem.' She had a buoyant, matter-of-fact confidentiality which was an effective technique in drawing out someone who was dwelling too much in themselves.

'Well before we start,' I quipped, 'do you prefer private or public care, or payment in kind?'

'Do you want an answer before or after I pick up the scissors?' she said with a wicked-eyed gaze into the mirror.

One of the pleasing things about talking to a hairdresser is that you can see her and what she is doing while the conversation progresses. That is not always the case when you are positioned by the doctor. Perhaps surgeries should have eye contact mirrors placed on the walls near the examination couches so that patients can maintain conversational contact with their doctor. 'Not too short, it's winter,' I pleaded.

'Well now,' she said, starting the warm wash. 'My boyfriend and I have to go to an "Australia Party" dressed as an Aussie couple and I'm buggered if I know what to wear.'

'Hmm,' I said as her breasts accidentally brushed across my arm.

'What do you think?' she quizzed.

'Well, whatever it is, it should match your personality.'

'That's what I think,' she said. 'But it has to be a double match and Mr Plod wants to go as something to do with cricket—and where would that leave me?'

She had the scissors around my ears so I decided against my suggestion to go as a streaker.

'He's a bit of an athlete is he?' I asked.

'Physical first, second and third,' she said in a rather tired tone.

'OK,' I said with sudden inspiration as I looked at the

reflection of this big, healthy, bold eyed blond in the mirror. 'You go as Lisa Curry, champion Aussie swimmer, and Mr Muscle can go as iron-man boyfriend Grant Kenny.'

'Brilliant,' she said. 'You're not just a busted body.'

'Will you go in a speedo costume?' I asked closing my eyes.

'Plus towel to start with,' she said laughing.

'One of *those* parties, eh?' I said with nostalgia.

I always went to the same salon and Heather always cut my hair. Like so many hairdressers she was a storyteller and had insatiable curiosity.

'Mate of mine broke a leg skiing last week,' she said, starting on the top of my head. 'And they've put this bloody great metal scaffolding thing on her leg. Christ it's ugly. Why didn't they put on a plaster?' she asked, tapping mine with her comb.

Once again I thought how much we doctors take for granted the knowledge we have but which our patient's lack. 'It varies with the fracture,' I said.

'Do tell,' she called from around the back of my head.

'Well, fractures are treated according to three basic principles—the three R's: *reduction* of the fractured bones to their normal alignment and position—usually under anaesthetic; *retention* of the bones in that position using any of a number of methods; and then *rehabilitation* of the muscles and joints back to as full a function as possible.'

'Reduction and Rehab I understand,' she said. 'But why the metal contraption to retain it?'

'It depends on a lot of things: the actual bone broken; the nature of the fracture—whether it's shattered or just snapped, and whether it's compound or simple.'

'Like interest rates,' she said with a look of mock stupidity.

'Sorry. A simple fracture is one where the tissues over the broken bone are not penetrated. A compound fracture is one where the site of the actual break in the bone has had contact with the surrounding air, either through the bone penetrating the muscle and skin, or the original trauma lacerating the skin and muscle from the outside.'

'Sounds horrible.'

'Yes, but the importance of a compound or open fracture is that contamination and then infection is a possibility and the surgeon is less inclined to put in any foreign material.'

'Foreign material?'

'Yes, like metal screws, plates, rods or wires.'

'Why?'

'Because if you get infection around foreign material, the body can't get rid of the infection as long as the metal or whatever is in the body. It can grumble on and produce inflammation in the bone or osteomyelitis.'

'Then how come you have a plaster on your broken leg and she had the external contraption?'

'She had the best of it,' I said. 'My left leg fracture was compound. The bone went through my leg and I had a deep gash where the gear stick did the same. The risk of infection would have been too great to fix the bones with an external metal scaffold fixateur.'

'OK, then why do you say she had the best of it? She said she would rather have had a nice clean white plaster.'

'If she had, then she wouldn't have been able to move her knee or ankle. See'—I pulled up the leg of my track suit pants—'the joints are fixed by the plaster. You can only retain a fracture in its correct position with a plaster if you immobilise the joint above and below the fracture. So for a break in the main shin bone—the tibia—the plaster must extend from just below the groin to just above the toes.'

'I see. You're right—she can move her knee and ankle.'

'And so she avoids a lot of muscle wasting, joint stiffness and even the danger of blood clots in the leg from immobility. The scaffold of metal is suspended by screw rods which go into the bone above and below the fracture and are then united by a cross bridge. Provided the rod sites are kept clean and antiseptic, the result is just as good as with a plaster and the rehabilitation is much quicker.'

'So you didn't have any metal put in?'

'Not in the left leg, but I did in the right.'

'Don't tell me—because it was a different fracture?'

'Top of the class,' I said.

'Teacher's pet?' she said with a twinkle.

'If only I were younger,' I said.

'You're still active, old boy.'

'My ankle is the only part of me that's been screwed recently,' I quipped.

'Ho, ho, ho,' she said applying the hot hair dryer to my bare neck.

'And why screws?'

'The right ankle was a real mess. The whole joint had been ripped apart, most of the ligaments ruptured and the fractures in the bones had gone right through into the smooth joint surfaces.'

'Bad news, huh?'

'Yes. Unless the surgeon can get the bones back together accurately, the joint surface will be rough and then they will wear and tear as you use the ankle and will eventually produce osteoarthritis in the joint. The screws fix the fractures internally and help them to heal and unite in the correct position.'

'So the screws stay in?'

'Some do, but some come out after the bones have united. Two of mine are out and I think one or two are still in to help maintain cohesion in the joint because all the ligaments were stuffed.'

'You've been through quite a bit mate,' she said brushing me down and handing me my crutches.

'Yeh,' I said, paying her and then moving as quickly as I could into the street to avoid a display of emotion which always seemed to rush through me whenever strangers showed me any tenderness.

The first time I went to lay in the sun on the sand I was alone and sat away from everyone on a beach I had never visited before. My crushed and thrombosed left leg was a thick, unrecognisable twin to its partner. But their brotherhood was identified in their similar scars. I was glad to peel off the tight support stocking to let the skin feel the sun.

The leg had done its best: it had healed and it was whole. My job was to accept it. I covered the scars with sun block cream for the first occasion of what would become a lifelong ritual. I didn't swim and was shy of walking the beach with a wasted, sagging body. But it was a first step; and in any recovery it is the courage needed for the first step in any tentative direction which is the most elusive and important.

After the first successful step has been taken, frequently a recovering patient pushes forwards with a defiant belligerence before he draws back into a more measured stride. Only acceptance can assist this process. I went through a phase where I was determined not to be ashamed of my damaged body.

I forced the issue by going to the nude beach at Sunnyside—
and came home with a burnt bum.

At least the gymnasium overcame one source of despair.
I remember the sheer horror and disgust I felt at seeing the
degree to which my legs had wasted after thirteen weeks in
plaster. The loss of flesh was appalling. My shoulder was a
scaffold of bone, my thighs and calves were mere sacks of skin
and my neck and arms hung as though they existed only to
prove the theory of gravity.

While I have always tried to practise medicine from the
patient's point of view, the experience of my own recovery
taught me many things about illness which no amount of
abstract sympathy could have achieved and which no textbook
ever mentioned. One of them was how unprepared most patients
are for the sight of their damaged body—the scars, the wasted
limbs and the flaking, ugly skin.

While I couldn't do much with the muscles the gym helped
me develop, at least I did not need to hide my body from
myself or others. It also helped me in my lifelong battle with
my weight. Following the accident, as my strength returned,
I became gravely concerned about the steady increase on the
scales, made worse since I couldn't participate in major exercise.
To have to return to the drudgery of an endless diet was like
facing hell.

Prior to the accident, every form of weight-loss endeavour
had ultimately failed. Fasting, diets, sugar-free food, Weight
Watchers, proprietary diet foods, health farms and fads had
all been tried and found unhelpful. It was only when I added
physical activity which used 2,000 calories a day that I was
able to combine my erratic eating with exercise to produce
a reasonably stable weight. With my particular inventory of
injuries, especially to my ankles and shoulder, running, squash,
windsurfing and the gym were all beyond me because of the
impact forces on my joints. And at that time I was still not
able to manage the joy of my bicycle. Even before the gym
closed for Christmas, my attendance had become half-hearted.
I still tried to do some exercises each day but I lacked genuine
motivation because I had reached physical barriers I could not
cross without causing additional damage.

The human mind has an almost infinite capacity to
rationalise adversity so I slipped into a justification of physical

disinterest with ease. I convinced myself that fitness and athleticism were impermanent and wasteful. I decided I should be doing something *really* stimulating—like reading or writing or exploring new parts of the world.

I didn't realise when I started on my trek of recovery just what a mirage physical improvement could be. It does not always partner the inner healing. Quite the opposite. The external signs of physical improvement can make a casual observer believe recovery is more complete than it is. This experience made me realise something important: that the subconscious tendency for an accident victim to exaggerate a limp or to accentuate a grimace, arises not from the desire to win sympathy, or to inflate a compensation claim, but rather to hold back signs of physical improvement so they match the shorter strides of emotional repair.

There was little point in pushing things past agony. Initially I was prepared to endure pain and it didn't restrict or affect me in the way others thought it might as I tried to push the physical restrictions further and further away. But the delights I experienced during the day, as I strove to move back the physical barriers, were matched equally by the restrictions produced at night by the consequences. It was no joy to defiantly run a few hundred metres on shattered ankles and to pass through pain barriers only to be unable to limp to the bathroom the following morning.

The time came when I was forced to acknowledge that I had to draw back from my desire to confront the limitations caused by the injuries. That was a difficult thing for me to do. It was the first time in my life that my mental drive had been thwarted by a physical restriction. I had to acknowledge that my wilful efforts to improve my strength and fitness were actually adding damage to my body.

Without realising it, in reducing the importance of my physical endeavours I was removing the only remaining barrier between me and a full confrontation with the emotions I had been unable to face.

15

DESPAIR

Forgive me if I've shunned so long
Your gentle greeting, earth and air!
Yet sorrow withers e'en the strong
And who can fight against despair!

Emily Brontë

There is a limit to the number of changes a human being can make at any one time. There is a breaking point for us all. Anyone who has been ill, severely injured, or suffered major emotional stress should be cautious about changing jobs, homes or partners all at the same time.

Some of the strongest human beings I've known seem to have managed these events, and while they have been a source of inspiration to me I know that for many of them their sense of hollowness has taken an eternity to heal.

The time came when I did not want to talk about the accident at all. It happened when the rate of my recovery was so slow that I was overwhelmed by the frequency with which I was meeting people I hadn't seen since the smash. At that time I could only mumble ambiguous half-truths like, 'I am coming along,' or 'It's improving slowly'.

But inside me a voice screamed, 'Please stop asking!' 'Please go away!' 'Please leave me in peace!'

I wanted to be alone.

My grief was like my pain: both caused isolation because they were intensely personal. I knew that unless I turned them around through my inner resources or the support of my friends, they would crush my body, cripple my mind and destroy my spirit. Things which crush the body are brutal; those which damage the mind are sinister, but those which destroy the spirit are evil. The full consequences of the accident had the power to do all three.

This period of my experience of recovery is still painful to touch and had I not kept the small notebook from those months I'm not sure I would be able to share it. Eight months after the accident, following a complete loss of confidence at home, and a crisis of personal relevance, I wrote:

> I am now in a prison. It is worse than that Kafka-like state where one feels jailed without explanation by an unknown force. In my present internment not only are the crimes unidentified and the warder anonymous, but the actual elements of restraint are abstract.
> What is the shackle? Is it simply a submissive exhaustion like the weariness felt by a long-serving prisoner weakened by neglect—an enfeeblement which robs him of the strength to get up and be free even if the restraining bars are removed? Is it because I know subconsciously that I do not have the energy needed to sustain an escape? Can one be a fugitive on the run with two broken legs?
> Or is it because I believe escape from the confinement I wish to be rid of will create even greater damage than I suffer now?
> Perhaps to admit that I need to escape from a self-made situation is too great an admission of my shortcomings. I hope it is only a matter of strength, healing and time before I manage to face the long-term consequences of the accident.

There is a limit to the damage a human being can absorb. Perhaps the relatives and friends of injured people do not always realise how damaging additional stresses are to the victim. It feels as though someone is shifting the finishing line of a marathon further and further away as one stumbles towards it exhausted and bereft.

> I am so tired, so incapable and unwilling to do battle of any sort. My only option is to become quiet and withdrawn—it's the only way to cope. I must subtract all personal involvement from any additional stresses and

leave them behind me. On days like this, I feel that if anyone gave me a push I would drop and not just hit the ground but go on falling forever. The accident has made me aware in the worst way that it is far easier to kick a human being who is down than to hit him.

Just as I cannot offer damaged goods and retain my reputation in the market place of life, so I should not offer a damaged self. I will just withdraw. I know people are seeing it as self-indulgent but how can anyone else know how much a person who is suffering needs to be indulged. All joys seem to have vanished. That is the worst damage that has been done. I have no appetite for the new adventure. I feel alone.

I do not wish to apologise for setting down the horrible contractions which the accident inflicted on my life. The selfishness of sickness is a matter of survival. To brighten it up would be an unforgivable lie.

The feeling that people were thinking I 'ought' to be improving and moving on away from thoughts about myself only made things worse. Patients can do without additional feelings of failure when trying to recover.

I wonder how many people around me are aware of how much I am 'brave-facing' my plight. Can they sense how close I am to the edge, or how much effort is needed to keep up the appearance of coping with this relentless mess?

One bizarre motive for this sham was to regain some control over my life through an attempt to hide the real experience from the world. The accident removed the chance for me to determine my life. When everyday events caused further erosion of my self-determination, it was tempting to surrender completely from the fight. It was the only time in my life when suicide seemed a solution.

The more intensely and totally an individual has controlled a life in the way I had, the greater the consequences of the loss of that control and the greater the crisis of resentment. There were times after the accident when I felt so angry I would have wrecked the universe had I been able. That sort of anger makes you feel hideous and degraded; it makes you want to damage things. But this period of my recovery showed me that being angry was preferable to being emotionally empty. The worst grief was the realisation of how great an influence my reduced inner life exerted over all my outside interests— which evaporated completely. For months I was busy without direction, talked without purpose, sat without peace and walked without a destination. It was not me. Some days I wished I could have been reintroduced to the world. I wondered who all the people were and what they meant.

I believe that all those who have suffered severe physical or emotional pain sense that their recovery has rushed them through too many feelings and experiences in too short a time. And unless one is on guard, ill health and a driving desire to recover can rip the soul from a man. He becomes his body and is only physical.

It was at this time and in this deadened emotional state that I wrote a note of bold agreement with H. G. Wells' sentence:

> My children mean much to me in friendliness, interest and happiness, but they do not go deeply into the living structure of myself. Sons and daughters nowadays are still an intimate part of one's pride, a projected part of one's persona, but are no more part of one's inner shadow than is the general world of acquaintances and friends.

When my emotional sanity was restored and my emotional survival was assured, Wells' words were like a foreign language without relevance to the sentiments I held for my children. The emotional depletion imposed by my battle to survive greatly distorted the feelings in my heart.

A little over a year after the accident a page towards the end of my notebook recorded the following:

> In any life there are elements of joy and despair which involve family, friends and work. While they all interweave with the experience of severe injury, they will not be the primary focus of these notes.
> The events which stood inside will be mentioned only as they relate to recovery, not of themselves.

Like most of my writing at that time, it is almost illegible, even to me. Now, in 1991, I am completely puzzled by the phrase, 'stood inside'. Perhaps it was 'look inside', or 'struck inside'.

The self-concern which I felt at that time was true. That was the reality of the distortion of my world when I viewed it through the prism of my recovery. At the grey end of a colourless spectrum most of my life was filtered through a self-regarding light.

But if my account of this period causes some human waste to be avoided by helping others survive their assaults, and if the many patients and families who have suffered road accidents gain some strength from my shared experience, it will have done its work. In all this my hope has been that some elements of my recovery will be recognised as true by the many others who had suffered a significant injury. I know how inappropriate it would be to stray into generalisations which were foreign to the experience and recovery of others.

My confidence in having something meaningful to share was affected each time I was confronted by the ways in which my experience was different from many of my co-sufferers: the accident had not been my fault; no-one else had been injured—in particular no-one had been damaged by me; I faced no potentially punitive legal proceedings; I suffered no head or spinal injury and no confronting disfigurement; the operations and healing were free of complications; the accident produced no loss of job or basic earning capacity and no enduring impairment of my social functions, or any unwelcome social stigma. Furthermore, as a doctor, my personal perspective of the events of recovery had the benefit of my professional background. I was spared both the ignorance and fear often experienced by many patients. I knew my prognosis as accurately as those caring for me. I understood the reasons why things were done or requested by the treating staff. And, apart from two or three occasions, I was neither intimidated nor patronised by hospital staff.

In all of these things my experiences were somewhat different. And yet, beneath it all I felt a bond of understanding with the most basic feelings of that huge number of Australians whose bodies have been damaged and whose emotions have been torn on the roads. I knew in my heart my experience was united with theirs.

Something happened the other day which helped me feel

the strength of that common bond. A big ruckman type of lad who had rolled a truck and splintered quite a few bones the year before was attending my clinic for review of his progress. Physically he had achieved a great deal within the limitations of his injuries. And yet, as we discussed the fine improvements he had made and his future treatment programme, he did not look at me.

I didn't persist with my encouragement. I simply said 'It's horrible when the body is doing its job, but nothing feels like it's healing inside'.

The big bloke looked up and gazed straight into my eyes as if to say, 'How did you know that?'

I said quietly, 'I've been there, Billy, and what puzzled me was why it all felt like it was falling to pieces inside me eight to nine months after the accident. I wondered if I had exhausted myself in getting my body to where I had.'

You don't often see a six foot, five inch, twenty-four year-old Australian cry in front of a stranger, even when the stranger is his doctor. It did us both good.

16
LATER THOUGHTS

To believe your own thought, to believe
That what is true for you in your
Private heart is true for all men ...

Ralph Waldo Emerson

The advice the rehabilitation team gave me when I left Hampton Hospital was that I should continue my morning gymnasium exercises to improve strength and mobility, and do lots of walking in the afternoons. They also stressed I should not rush back to work before my endurance was stronger.

Walking was essential because it was the only exercise I could manage for the sustained period necessary to build my stamina. I walked for hours along the suburban bayside beaches, resting frequently, as needed, to ease the muscle cramps and pain. And sometimes while sitting on the sand looking across Port Phillip Bay I experienced moments of peace and privacy so different from the loneliness I felt when I was with other people. The thoughts I had in those quiet times helped to turn around the despair of the previous months. They also helped to make my spirits stronger and many things clearer in my mind.

My first positive thoughts were those of gratitude to the people who had helped me recover to this stage: the ambulance men who had reached the accident in under six minutes; the police who cleared the traffic chaos; the staff in the hospitals; the generous people who donated the blood which helped to keep me alive; the nurses who provided such tender care; and my family and friends. They all made me feel I was worth preserving. They also gave me courage to reclaim the being I was, the individual who preceded the person who was the 'son', 'husband', 'father', 'friend', or 'doctor'. He was, to use Gide's phrase, 'the original Adam', free of everything which had been imposed on him or expected of him.

I understood that I was not simply the sum of the external expectations which had accumulated with each label. None of us are. We exist as primary beings with a fundamental obligation to live true to our essence. My basic allegiance was simply to reflect my own reality. There was nothing opinionated in that: we are all special cases. And there was nothing selfish in it either: most of us contribute best to others when we feel comfortable with ourselves.

I realised that all titles or labels unnerved me. They imposed certainty, confinement and stasis. They all acted against my freedom to be ambiguous, complex and total. They all forced me to play a part and reduced my chance to be approximate, changeable and interconnected—the trio of norms in nature.

Before the accident it was an almost impossible battle for me to preserve my right to express the odd aspects of my being in my work, interests and play. But after the smash, having nearly lost my life, I felt I had been given a second life. And as recovery progressed, I gained enough strength to firmly claim this second life as my own.

I became less inclined to be drawn into social shams or games. I tried to avoid situations which had the potential to require a ritual response or a prefabricated emotion divorced from the truth of the moment. Courtesy can be corrupting if it is everything. So can charm and style. There is a peculiar form of emotional integrity which refuses to subscribe to imposed human expectations. Mine flashed into action at unexpected moments during recovery. One involved a 'good friend'.

Joel Evans and I had been in the same class at high school, then in medical school together; and we had been involved with each other's weddings. We both became surgeons and had often shared warm company in each other's homes. Joel had not made any contact with me during the months of my recovery and our first meeting, almost a year after the accident, occurred by chance in a bookshop. He was very uneasy. 'How are you now?' he asked.

'OK,' I replied, disinclined to offer any personal details.

'Sorry I didn't visit you in hospital,' he said, looking over my shoulder.

'Your decision,' I said flatly.

'I wanted to, but every time something would crop up and—'

'Joel,' I interrupted. 'I can accept your indifference but I can't accept your bloody bullshit hypocrisy. You did what you wanted to—you cop the consequences. I was in hospital for months. I was surprised and hurt that you made no contact. Don't bullshit me with "I wanted to but I was too busy" crap. People less close to me than you flew in from interstate to make a visit.'

We went our own ways then, and have since. It's a waste of effort to try to provide both sides of the energy needed to support a friendship. Some things have to be shed in order to progress.

During recovery there were many occasions when the importance of the various elements in my life were reviewed and rethought.

In a curious way, it was comforting to know I could choose when to die—when to take up the option to leave the stage of life through the side door. That is a decision available to all of us unless we met a sudden and random death through calamities such as acute illness, violence or accidents.

Strangely, those of us who survive such events often carry an unusual burden. Having reached a 'near end' we feel a dual indignation: on the one hand that our life was nearly lost; and on the other that our option to choose when to die was almost removed. It is a load which undermines our faith in both the tenure of life and our primary right to resign from it. And it can contribute to sleeplessness, feelings of deep fatigue and an edgy despair. You can never be too sure. That is the frightening part of having been embraced by death. The touch tells you how easy it is to die. The gap over the grave widens: so easy to drop through.

A common belief among my friends was that life should be more precious to those who survive. But my feeling was that life had always been precious and that the major effect of the accident was to show in the starkest way how transient and tenuous the privilege of life could be. Rather than life being cherished more, I lived it more intensely. I felt a desire to celebrate each moment by making it live, by being in the day and attending to it.

As I watched the endless wash of waves over the sand during one of my walks, I realised that one could not kill time without injuring eternity. I needed to be absorbed in the given.

The accident also changed my feelings about immortality. I began to believe that it had only one dimension: the echoes of the energy I radiated to the world around me. It was my simple responsibility to try to make most of my energy contribute to a positive harmonic. On balance, the energy I released should take the larger rhythms just a tiny bit closer to unity. If, on the other hand, my personal contribution increased the combative, negative and damaging disharmonics, my life would have very little calmness or inner strength in itself, and its influence on the lives which came after me would be a legacy of conflict and confusion.

Before the accident my view of immortality was very different. I believed it could only exist in the minds of others through a direct influence, or indirectly through exposure to a lasting creation or record of actions. It was a less comprehensive understanding than the one I hold now. At that earlier time, I thought the greatest degree of immortality was created by those whose influence on others was widespread, intense and enduring. In that sense, Christ was very much alive but then so were Julius Caesar, Beethoven, Shakespeare, Buddha, Hitler and Presley.

But gradually, during the time I spent in solitude, I came to feel that there was nothing essential in Caesar's life which was not in my own or any one else's. The immortality available to each of us was larger than that which was restricted to human consciousness. It went beyond our influences on family or friends, factors which could gradually fade in the generations like a grave overgrown with weeds. It went further than those of our enduring works or original thoughts which may have been recorded in the memory of history.

I know it is an unusual sentiment, but now I feel that important elements of immortality will exist even if left 'unrecorded'. The beauty of the ballet dancer remains forever in the whole, even if it was never captured on film; the sounds of a singer remain in the wind even though they were never recorded; all gentle or cruel human actions leave their impact even if history books have missed them. Not a single grain of emotional sand can shift without affecting the moral universe.

During a moment of intense stillness I understood that human documentation was of small relevance to ultimate influences. So were word-of-mouth, human ritual or custom. I knew there was no profanity in my feeling that Christ did not need the Bible. The purest form of our immortality related simply to the content and direction of the energy which each of us had contributed to the whole. All the rest was simply the result of the efforts of busy advertising managers.

This understanding of immortality now helps me to remember who I am in all the actions I undertake, and not only those filtered for public presentation and observation.

While I had no desire for immortality I did feel the need to accept the challenge of trying to make some meaning out of the matrix of my life.

There had been earlier brief moments in hospital when the possibility of my death—and especially its consequences for who would care for my mother—filled me with indignation. During the time when I was upset in the ward, I had asked my friends, 'What would have been lost from the world had I been killed?' and had wondered how my own idea of the answer would measure with the responses of those who knew me well. Perhaps unfairly, considering my particular emotional state at that time, the closeness of their answers to my own perception became a crude measure in my mind of their understanding of my relevance as a human being, and of how close I felt to them. One thing was certain: that the characteristics which were most important to me, were often seen by others as traits which were difficult for them to understand or accommodate. Perhaps it would have been the same for me with my limited perception of their personalities. I certainly would have been wary if an acquaintance had asked me the same question about themselves.

Later on, during my strengthening walks, the possibility of my death became an intensely personal issue for me. The mood of my thoughts on what would be lost was different. It was rather a personal confrontation with that question and the realisation that the answer would sharply define what it was that I contributed in the larger sense. When I was alone, I believed that had I been killed a few special things would have been lost from the world. In my healing mind, they were capacities rather than achievements which mattered most. These included emotional intensity, resilience, a capacity for freedom, a life as an example of personal liberty, a passionate commitment to tasks, a power to focus energy, an ability to move an audience with a talk, an expansiveness, an ability to cross conventions and bridge barriers, imagination and creativity, a desire to care in an abstract way, a need to embrace widely, an enthusiasm for and commitment to the moment, and a debunking disrespect expressed through humour and fun. If they could be summarised as a single quality, it would be called energetic audacity.

The question of what would be lost from the world if one did not exist, is as profound as any a human being can ask themselves; and the honest answer is as close as they can come to an admission of who they see themselves to be. The ease with which one human being can ask another this question is a fair measure of the real comfort felt in their company.

Why was it that I felt so tentative about asking my family this question? Because I didn't want to confront the prospect of me being lost to them or them from me? Because they had already endured the prospect of that loss and should be spared further pain? Because a family should not be treated like friends? Or because I feared their answer? Tiredness and fear did not help to make easy answers.

Some of my children's experiences came back to me years later when I re-read the letters they had sent to me in the ward and when my wife told me about their early feelings.

David, my eldest son, was concerned that I had died and that the claim I was too ill to visit in intensive care was a pretence to keep the truth from the children. David loves in gentle ways.

John could not understand why it had happened to his father; the youngest of the children, he was filled with dire thoughts about the driver who struck me. He saved his meagre pocket allowance and bought me a bedside momentum toy whose spheres swung in rhythmical pendulum arcs. I managed to tangle the strings while he was there, and mercifully I was able to untangle them before he reached home to receive a message that Dad had retrieved the situation.

Ceri, who had a deep understanding of the enforced loneliness I was enduring in the ward, expressed great tenderness in her notes to me. Ceri had a Jane Austen eye for detail and finely developed instincts for psychological pain even though she was only fifteen years-old.

Tristyn, my youngest daughter, was always positive, encouraging and buoyant. Her outward expressions did not always match her private feelings. Like her father, the face could smile while the soul hurt.

At the time of the accident I felt closer to my younger children. Now I feel closer to the elder pair. No doubt, as in most families, it will change again.

I will never know even a fragment of what the children felt during those perilous early weeks. Their pain is private. But I do know that their will for me to live helped to turn the tide of my recovery towards survival.

The threat to my life in the early weeks also made me reaffirm my life-long resolve never to leave my children fatherless as I had been left. That resolve was also a source of power for my will to survive. Now, at a time when I am recovered to the maximum possible level, my personal contract has been achieved, for they are no longer children.

What else was really important? How did one determine that? There are times in a life when one has a good clear out or a clean up: if you change jobs all the files are culled; if you finish a major task or a relationship your room is tidied; if you change house the address book is revised and the wardrobe subjected to the ten year test—if it hasn't been worn for years give it to the Salvation Army. I had the same feeling following the accident except it was my life which needed a revision. During these clear outs I sometimes found things which revealed the way the accident and its injuries had changed me, and at those moments I felt sadness, resignation and occasionally a sense of surprise.

During the relaxed week between Christmas and New Year, nine months after the accident, I had the chance to sort some papers, and while sifting through folders I discovered the outline of a speech I had been drafting three years earlier. Compared with my weakened spirits, I was struck by how vigorous and positive its thoughts were. The context of them was intriguing because they revealed a rough portrait of some of my ideas at that time. And they gave me a clear view of how the accident had buried those perspectives.

The theme of this particular speech was 'Don't prescribe pills for personal problems' or 'Valium is no substitute for self-respect'. It was a plea for doctors to tear up their prescription pads when it came to the treatment of emotional or inter-personal problems. In their place it encouraged them to ask individual patients to assess all the major factors and influences in their lives and determine the extent to which an activity or involvement trivialised them. It suggested we should ask of each ingredient in a troubled life, 'Does this thing make me less than I know I am? Does it subtract from my individual potential? And if it does, shouldn't I discard it, or at least revalue my involvement with it?'

It also suggested that human fulfillment and harmony, and a diminishing need for pharmaceutical support, could only occur if an individual felt the privilege of their existence: if they appreciated the uniqueness of their capacity to learn, to create, to be affectionate, to imagine, to be curious and, at the end of the day, to feel that the world meant more to them as a result of their efforts, no matter how modest those efforts were to the rest of the world. It made the point that there is a mountain of difference between the worldly importance of something and its importance to an individual. It stated rather boldly that all institutions were a potential source of damage to an individual's self-respect. Structures including schools, work, marriage, clubs, societies, social pretensions, politics and that noisy enemy the media, could all reduce an individual's power to feel and realise their own potential.

Looking back, the speech felt as though it had been written by someone else, but stranger than that, it felt as though its message had been tailored for my own strengthening state of mind. If all things are meant to be and are part of a larger purpose in which we participate, then that scruffy draft helped to clear away some of the things which were hindering my emotional recovery.

In most of our lives, at any time, our degree of personal

contentment will vary. For most of us there are many potential sources of unhappiness and, for a few, a significant struggle with internal fragmentation. Our relationships, our work or our feelings of unfulfillment can all contribute to our sense of having a blemished life.

From my experience in partnering patients, I know these feelings of failure have many causes which can make up a brewing stew of human sourness. They include ambitions beyond ability; character traits like laziness or habitual feelings of inadequacy which subvert human potential; impractical, unrealistic or impossible expectations of oneself or others; inadequate opportunities; being thwarted by others; public humiliation; bad luck and misfortune, and many others, including sheer exhaustion of effort and the associated sense of surrender. It is not surprising that the convenience of blaming incidental injuries or illnesses for feelings which ought to be linked to their real cause can be too attractive for some to resist. Every fluctuation of mood towards unhappiness, every event which causes dispirited feelings, every down day, can be blamed on the injury.

I've seen patients who have blamed their accident for all the enduring trouble and turmoil in their lives and who have loaded their relatives or their compensation claims with this unrelated and incidental unhappiness. And I've seen others who have had no desire to use the accident in this way. But whatever the individual capacities of severely injured people to cope with their troubles, we are all united in this: the superimposed effects of the accident always undermines our ability to cope with the other stresses of our lives and can lead us to cry, 'I have had enough!'

17
BODY HARMONY

There is nothing the body suffers
the soul may not profit by.

George Meredith

I heard him crying behind the cubicle curtain in the hydrotherapy pool change room. With a late morning review appointment at the surgeon's rooms I had left the pool session early
to get dressed, and had expected to find the change room
empty.

As I sat down and drew the curtain to protect my own
privacy I could hear his muffled sobs nearby. Not wanting to
be intrusive, I tried to help as best I could by sending him
my silent concern. But when he wailed a really anguished sound
I went around and asked him if he was OK.

He was sitting in his tracksuit, crying openly, with his head
back against the wall. I knew he was close to the edge. It
was the cry of a damaged man.

'Sorry,' he said remotely. 'I've just about had it. I was going
all right, but today I can't even get my shoes and socks off.'

He closed his eyes and was silent.

'Here,' I said kneeling unsteadily, 'let's see if we can get
them off.'

'Damn legs are a mess,' he said almost apologetically.

'The pool helps me when I feel like chucking it in,' I said.
'Do you want me to wait?'

'No,' he said. 'I'll try and get it together. I'm just tired of my body not working. It won't get better while I sit here.'

'Take care,' I said, closing his curtain.

I dressed, and as I waited for the taxi to drive me to my appointment I thought about the look on his face. A reliant thirty year-old man who was used to doing all the heavy physical work around his home, to jogging and enjoying his life, was facing the full force of his loss. He had been reduced to the level of a finger-clumsy three year-old who needed help with his shoes and socks. At least both of us were beyond the stage where we needed assistance with our personal care in the bathroom.

I knew he would be feeling better for the cry. Men need to cry more often than they do. It took me months and months before I could come out from crying behind curtains and doors. We hide too much.

I climbed into the taxi hoping that the two-way intercom was switched off and that the driver was not in a chatty mood.

'Big smash?' he asked, as I positioned the crutches beside me alongside the door.

'Big enough,' I said, trying to balance my disinclination to talk about it with a wish not to appear abrupt.

'Mate of mine had a bad one,' he started.

I turned to warn him from the subject and stopped when I saw the pain in his eyes. 'He's a real good mate,' he said with affection. 'Went through a windscreen. He was in a coma for a week, didn't know what was going on for a month and now they're trying to fix the scars on his face.'

'Could take some time,' I said.

'Yeh, they've done quite a few operations already and they've put these pressure bandages on. Seems funny to put pressure on a scar.'

I was at the crossroads of the conversation. Silence and anonymity, or the prospect of a medical tutorial. I compromised. 'From what some of the patients tell me the pressure bandages are to keep the scar still and free of tension and that allows it to heal in a way which produces the least ugly result. The scar is finer and flatter.'

'Oh good, I'll tell him that later today,' he said, happy at the prospect of being able to relay some good news to his friend.

I could have shown him the scars on my shoulder, chest,

legs or ankles to complete the lesson, but I was happy with his satisfaction. The scar on my shoulder would have been a good illustration of the principles of wound healing.

Whenever the body is damaged it responds with inflammation, irrespective of whether the source of that damage is a physical blow, a cut, an infection, or the result of chemical, electrical or thermal burns. What happens then depends on the nature and extent of the damage. If it is not severe the inflammation can resolve and no lasting trace results—as with mild sunburn for example. But if the damage results in tissue being lost or any laceration deeper than an abrasion, then the inflammation will organise into a scar, or if it is inside the body cavities, into adhesions. These fibrous scars and adhesions are always permanent. Most frequently they cause no problems apart from cosmetic concerns if they are obvious. Occasionally the scars or adhesions can cause trouble. If they are sited around joints they can make them stiff and immobile, as was the case with my ankles; or if they occur in the chest they can stick the lung membrane to the chest wall and cause discomfort when you breathe deeply, which is what I experienced with any vigorous exercise.

Any operation on the abdomen can produce adhesions which occasionally cause the intestines to be kinked or twisted and produce severe pain. As bleeding is usually associated with damage, and blood is chemically irritating when it seeps into tissues, extravasation of blood can make the adhesions or scarring worse. And so can any superimposed infection. Gratefully, I was spared that complication.

But my shoulder scar was interesting because it was the result of two operations through the same scar. The first, to put in the pin across the joint between the collar bone (clavicle) and wing bone (scapula) after which the shoulder was held immobile for many weeks; and the second opening only the outer half of the scar to take out the pin and allow me to get the shoulder moving. The first part of the scar which had been protected by a pressure dressing and total immobilisation is a fine and almost undetectable line, while the second half is broad, raised and obvious as a result of my mobilising efforts on the shoulder and the consequent stretching of the scar.

That is why plastic surgeons always insist on immobilising the scars of cosmetic surgery. Those beauty considerations were the least of my concerns. I wanted clean, quick healing and the restoration of my body function. And I knew from my days in the operating theatre that a surgeon should never be shy of extending the incision an inch or two at either end if the operation is difficult and deep, because this allows greater access and visibility. I remembered what my surgical teacher had told me: 'It shouldn't matter how long you make an incision because physical wounds heal up from side to side, not end to end, and take the same time no matter how long they are'.

This is true. But the opposite is the case for emotional wounds. The longer and deeper they are the longer they take to heal. And they always leave a scar: the memory of feelings.

The injuries we suffer affect all aspects of our lives because each part of our bodies has its own particular functional task to do, but each has an additional emotional meaning. Injuries can damage both.

My body was such a silent machine. After the accident I noticed changes in its environment of inner sound.

Each of us knows the noises in our homes, street, or work. We register changes in the same way as we ignore the familiar. It's the same with our bodies. They are so silent. The humourists might quip, what about the chatterboxes and the coughers and the wind blowers? But that's not what I mean. I mean the silent efficiency of the machinery of the body. My body made sounds only when it contacted the outside world, via my foot steps or activities—even the scribble of a pen on paper. But the actual machine of my undamaged body was superbly silent. Moving my muscles, joints or limbs created no sound. That was why the addition of sounds to its internal silence were perceived so acutely. The creaks and rubs in my damaged joints, the crunches across malaligned ribs, or the ringing in my ears were reminders that my body was not tuned perfectly. They were the physical representation of the internal takeover by the emotional intruder.

As I watched the other patients recovering, I became increasingly aware of the emotional elements of our anatomy. Our legs are the supporting columns of the body and the basis of our mobility, and the damage done to one's 'emotional body' by leg injuries relates to this dual function. One feels unsupported and immobile, influencing fundamental feelings of strength, stability and involvement. Our arms and hands allow us to do creative and personal things and to communicate by gesture and touch. We can feel a sense of emotional muteness, an inability to make contact, when they are damaged.

My arms and legs were injured but it was the damage to my ribs and lungs which carried the greatest emotional significance, extending beyond the physical damage to my chest. I was prepared for the restricted activity imposed by the discomfort of breathing deeply, but my inability to sigh or stretch freely was completely unexpected. They were such pleasurable things to do and so simple, I felt it was unfair that they should be taxed with discomfort. The sustained feeling of being bound around the chest, of having my basic breathing rhythms in a strait jacket of pleural pain symbolised the involuntary restraint imposed on my life in general. It was as though I was denied a basic freedom: to take air and breathe freely.

My relationship with my body became more intense following the injuries. There was a greater appreciation of things I had previously taken for granted, particularly the significance of the injuries to my responses, and my understanding of an altered sense of self.

A sensitive awareness of the emotions assisted by various bits of our bodies was an important insight for me to gain and one which is often lacking in those involved with caring for injured people because of shortcomings in our clinical apprenticeship and education.

Some effects of injury are obvious. The impact of damaged hands on a musician or technician, of disrupted knees on a sports player, of a disfigured face or body on a public figure, of a depleted voice on a teacher or receptionist, are all immediate and observable. Other consequences can affect the projected image or stature of an individual, the judge who suffers a stroke, the surgeon who cannot stand, an athletics coach restricted to a wheelchair, or a policeman with a limp. But a third level is how the injuries affect the specific emotional fabric of an individual's life: its freedom, mobility, power, contact, intimacy and participation in all their whimsical, eccentric, capricious and strange expressions.

The same injuries can affect all three territories of human existence. People do not use their legs simply to move from one place to another. They use them emotionally as well as physically to stay in contact with a group of people or a friendly conversation, to join a moment of joy, or to follow someone they want to shout at. When I was immobile I felt a kind of impotence. The members of the family could move out of a room or friends could get up from a table leaving me sitting, static and bound. It was frustrating when a conversation I was enjoying got up and departed; and it was humiliating when people walked away from my feelings. Wheelchairs cannot go up the steps of human insensitivity. I could not protect my sanity simply by leaving stressful situations: by moving out of a room full of animosity or dispute, by leaving a meeting place full of irrational rancour, or by storming off to a space where my anger could collect itself. My physical injuries made me vulnerable and often left me feeling exposed.

While my irrational angers were often focused on my family and friends they were rarely directed at those providing my medical care. Almost uniformly the attention and treatment I received were of the highest standard. There were two or three exceptions which cast a hard contrast to the generally trouble-free care I received from the staff. I'll mention the exceptions, not to give them disproportionate dues, but simply to remind myself of medical blemishes I must strive to avoid in my own practice. Both were examples of deficiencies in human sensitivity and understanding rather than crass incompetence, although one bordered on neglect. And both occurred when I was immobile and could not easily separate myself from them.

One happened early in my recovery when I was attending a clinic for review. The young doctors concerned stood beside me discussing another patient as I lay looking at the ceiling. The human relation to surrounding space changes for an invalid. With gross incapacity we have a closer relationship with the floor and ceiling of a room when seen from a bed or wheelchair and decreased contact with the doors, windows and walls at hand.

'So you were hit by a truck,' said one.

'Yes,' I said, gazing at the corner angle of the room where three surfaces joined with perfect precision.

'I had a near miss once,' he replied.

'I had one last week,' said his colleague joining in a sort of 'near miss' show and tell.

'Came over a rise,' continued the first. 'Only doing eighty, and a great whacking truck on the wrong side of the road overtaking some other bugger. Just got back in time. It could have been very nasty,' he said, feeling the muscle wasting in my thigh with incidental interest. 'I felt like turning round and chasing after him to give him a serve. But I was shaking too much.'

'Mine happened on the Eastern Freeway last Tuesday,' continued the other. 'Which day were you hit?' he asked, turning his attention to me.

'Thursday,' I said with rising fascination.

'Mine was last Tuesday, busy traffic, wet road, all the lanes full and suddenly this monster with a hundred wheels changes lanes without so much as a hoot and nearly ploughs me into the next life. Really shook me up, I can tell you,' he said in a tone which expected my sympathy.

I remained silent.

'How long has this plaster been on now?' he asked vaguely.

'Five weeks.'

'Five. And then I watched him flying on at speed and thought, if you go on like that, mate, you'll finish up killing someone.'

'Or worse,' said the other.

'Worse?' I enquired, genuinely wondering how this keen medical mind worked.

'Yes, finish up making someone a vegetable.'

'I see,' I said.

'There are some maniacs out there,' he concluded.

And there are some strange people in here, I thought, still remaining silent.

The other occasion was less whimsical. Throughout the whole journey of recovery, one professional group stood above almost every other in consistently providing humane, practical and skilful care: the nurses. And that made the single exception such a shock.

I knew from my own medical experiences that demanding patients can be really tiresome, particularly when they are the healthiest of those being cared for. By temperament and design, I tried to do as much as I could for myself. Being bed-bound put severe limitations on that independence. There were many things I needed to do which required the help of others and the nurses offered that help in most cases—usually with speed and often with a smile.

One didn't. My name for her was 'the terroriser'. Her favourite remark was 'back in a minute'. Her usual action was back in thirty. She left you in limbo with tasks which were begun and then left incomplete. She delivered things and then left them just out of reach. She was careless, lazy and I really struggled not to believe she was overtly cruel.

'Here's some mail for you,' she said, putting them on the bedside trolley near the wall.

'Could you pass them to me please,' I asked wearily.

'You want me to read them too, I suppose,' she said, disappearing.

It went on like that, small attritious incidents. Nothing major, but like the irritations in an eroding relationship each incident was like hair in the mouth. Each time she came on duty the observation chart at the foot of my bed started to fragment.

Then one day she was gone. Each shift for almost two weeks I waited uneasily for her almost evil idea of nursing care to reappear. It wasn't until a week later, in a bed on the ward balcony, that I heard the full story.

Evidently she had been giving a dose of her disinterest to a bloke who had fallen from a building construction and had, from all accounts, quite a bit to be angry about. Her indifference apparently was the last straw, because when she took an eternity to return to his bedside with the promised toilet roll—which she had forgotten to deliver with the bed pan—he gave her hell's annointment. She resigned in a stink, so to speak.

Being immobile often eliminated my ability to separate myself from such stresses. Everyone needs a safe place, but when the safety of your inner self has been left on a road, when home is turbulent, when work is impossible, when you can't drive, and when friends are lost, the combination can make you feel there is nowhere to crawl that is safe.

At first the accident strengthened my belief in the goodness of human nature and reaffirmed my faith in human kindness. But as the events of recovery progressed, I understood the actions of others more in terms of a return to me of the energy I had directed towards them. The good energies I had given I got back. Those I had not given I was made to suffer for. It had its own inherent fairness. I could not complain.

The man I had assisted in the hydrotherapy change rooms spoke to me quietly at morning tea the following day. 'Thanks for yesterday,' he said.

I answered with a simple touch to his forearm. Our injuries had been similar, but I didn't need to labour any understanding. Besides, tomorrow it could be me who needed his strength.

In any group or community of people the total amount of strength and shakiness remains pretty constant. It just moves to and fro like the happiness and hurt in an individual life.

18
PERSONAL CHANGES

*The world's a scene of changes, and to be
Constant, in nature were inconsistency.*

Cowley

I changed because of the accident. Some of the alterations were the directly enforced effects of the injuries. But the significant ones began during the time when my spirits reached rock bottom. The months of recovery provided the time for the changes to build their own strength.

For me, change was an extended process, not an event. It was geological, not meteoric. I had to dig to a great depth before I reached something of value.

The feeling which returned again and again was one of alteration. At first, the changes were all reductions. I felt that life had become restrained and restricted so that a sense of loss touched everything. The accident altered my opportunity to do the things which gave me pleasure and altered the pleasure provided by the things I was still able to do.

Late in my recovery this pervasive sense of loss was behind many outbursts of feelings at those times when I felt my life was being restrained still further. The decisions of doctors or the responses of family and friends which suggested I could not push forward on any frontier which I knew I could manage, produced distress. Someone doubted that I was 'safe' to go home from hospital and tried to hinder my release. I *was* ready and my willingness to fight the proposed delay in my parole showed clearly how ready I was. All accident victims feel that the next restriction is always 'the one too many'. We need reinforcement, not further constraints.

In the days before I accepted my new limitations, I could not think about alternatives. The contraction I felt was quite deadening. When I left the hospital all elements of my extroversion, joy and irreverent humour had been lost and replaced by a mood of solemn isolation. Never before in my life had I suffered in a way which made me doubt that my spirits would recover their strength. Then, very slowly, things started to change for the better.

> Before the accident he was outwardly friendly. That person was willing to go towards people, to encourage them, to joke, to entertain, flirt and infuriate. His social contact was marked by a mischievous willingness to throw conversational hand grenades and the courage to stand there and receive the blast. The desire to stir, prod and pry made him energetic and irritating company.

During the early period of my return to 'social life' there was a desire to avoid people and a confrontation with their questions, 'How are you?' and 'Are you getting better?' I tried to shun contacts by looking the other way, crossing the street or edging away from company. If I was caught I would try to turn the conversation away from the questions. I wasn't being discourteous or evasive. It was just that I didn't know how to answer. I wanted to be alone. But as time went on and some peace returned, my spectator activities began to bring some benefits.

> As an energetic, goal-orientated doer, the person who existed before the accident had rarely sat still. While this active and achieving way of life provided temporary and artificial respite from any confrontation with his significant personal blemishes, it also made the landscape of his life speed past in a blur.

With slowly growing strength, my social stillness provided an opportunity for a heightened awareness of the finer contents of the world. As a spectator I observed more than I did as an intrusive participant. Gradually, and with a progressive sense of relief, I became involved in the events around me. I noticed, absorbed and began to interact in a different, tentative and more gentle way.

I remember one occasion when I was waiting at a chemist shop counter for a prescription. In rushed a man exuding the sort of impatient irritation which made everyone edgy. Pushing in and creating waves of hostility among the other customers, it was no surprise that his anticipated photos were not ready. I had no desire to tick him off for pushing in or for his rudeness to the shop assistant. The whole scene was like watching a replay of the way I used to be. I watched the conflicting energy between his anger and the chemist assistant's diplomacy, and the associated rush of turbulence which departed with him and his self-generated frustrations. I knew he would drive, relate and live in the same disruptive way, against the grain of everything.

The assistant was visibly shaken. To help reduce the tension I sat down saying, 'I'm in no hurry, take your time,' and she replied with a smile in her eyes. I was pleased that I had not been the cause of the disruption and that in giving her some consideration my responses had avoided setting in motion some reverberating angers of my own.

My observations of everyday activities allowed me to notice subtleties of human interaction which previously I had overwhelmed. A good day was really only the progressive addition of a series of harmonious responses.

> Great in monologue, deficient in dialogue, that was the way he was. Too knowing to listen, too much in haste to pause. Prior to the accident he paid no heed to the sources of self-awareness offered by true conversations. The way he received the responses of others did not assist him in knowing himself. And as he shunned such knowledge because his emotional literacy was limited and because he had inadequate ways of revealing his pain, he was lost to the benefits of creative conversation and was invariably a vagrant listener.

Late in my recovery I began to listen to people, not to meddle with what they said, as I had, but to listen with interest and curiosity to try to gain a sense of shared experience or a new way of seeing.

I remember one day when I'd returned to the Royal

Melbourne Hospital for an outpatient appointment, meeting a nursing colleague from earlier years. The smile she greeted me with lacked conviction and the worries of her recent years showed in her eyes. It wasn't so much despair or pain, but rather a touch of bewilderment and surrender. Her voice was exhausted and suggested that easy answers to her problems had been very elusive. Her problem was not just the chaotic way her daughter was behaving—the rages and silences, the bitterness and withdrawal, epidemic in all teenage households— it was why she felt an overwhelming sense of personal guilt for this chaos. I listened for a long time, only speaking to ask if we could sit to take the weight off my ankles.

Perhaps her feelings were not much different from a generation of mothers who struggle to find a way to say, 'I love you, but . . .' to their adolescent children when they are doing their McEnroe impersonations. What was special for me was her comfort in telling me about some personal matters quite openly, and my disinclination to offer any advice. I felt strangely privileged to receive the confidences of people when they began to respond to my own altered ways. Perhaps they sensed that at last I'd been touched by my own troubles.

The accident also helped me to understand the importance of getting out of the way. Not in the obvious collisionary sense, but in the human sense.

> Before the smash he was always too large both physically and emotionally. As far as his family and friends were concerned he was often in their way, inhibiting, thwarting, suffocating, dominating, having his own way and wanting to run everyone's life. Like stuffy air, he filled the room so no-one could breathe easily. His life was like a game of poker. The hand he had been dealt was determined by the Gods. The way he played it was decided by his will, his skill, and his ability to bluff. His worst bluff was self-justification and the desire to blame someone else. These were the twin enemies of his growth and explained why at the age of forty-four he was still partly in emotional adolescence.

The accident began to break my habit of savage self-justification where my bristling indignation would sound and echo in a progressively perilous way. At first it was because

I didn't have the energy to battle with conflicts or arguments. Then, slowly through the process of disengagement and even early surrender, I realised that victory was not worth the bother. I did not need to be always right, to be first, to be successful, to be victorious, to be so relentlessly driven. And as I slowly shrugged free of these burdens, it became easier for me to say, 'Well done', 'Good idea', 'You are right', and 'What do you think?' Easier, but still not completely easy.

> The smash forced other changes to the way he lived. On the one hand he was audacious, reckless, irresponsible and carefree in an emotionally exploratory way. Sometimes he was a bit too dazzling for the darkness around him and for his own good. He was like a self-combusting star, shining his surface away. On the other hand he was disciplined, single-minded and intensely private.
> The two sides were united by the spirit of trying to live without regret. Like the soul in the Yevtushenko poem, when he died he wanted 'to fall down on the grass and die from the sheer joy of living'.
> 'I wish I had done that,' was not something he said often. The 'that' was nearly always done. Living was rich and alive in spite of occasional failures, wasted efforts, and some personal disarray. He believed that all people had the right to decide what would make them unhappy and to fail in their own way.

After the accident my life became more measured. A vigour for living was replaced by a tentative distrust because life had shown itself to be transient, whimsical and arbitrary. It had lost its sense of surety.

Once the physical rebuilding progressed and I re-entered a social world I was aware that the way I was relating in close friendship was also different.

> He had not been a naturally open person, outgoing but not confiding. Most contact, like most of his activities, had to be on his terms. The defect was more complex than that. He disliked familiarity, and was easily upset by people who presumed on his privacy. His abilities were significant personal barriers and he was easily bored with commonplace conversation. Worse than those flaws was

his will to control things so he could have his own way
and always be in the ascendancy.
He had always expected the world to work on his terms
and pushed to make it turn that way. Life was a strong
and self reliant pursuit and he often saw the people and
things around him as the means to that fulfillment.
Insofar as they complied with his design and assisted with
his personal orienteering, he was bothered with them.
He didn't have relationships he had arrangements. He
didn't have emotional bonds, he had exploiting
excursions. He didn't share himself, he had shares in
someone else's investment in him.

Why they stayed around this person was a mystery—I
wouldn't have put up with it. Perhaps I attracted people who
enjoyed the excitement of energy and unpredictability. Perhaps
they were responding to an obvious vulnerability.

All I can say now is that the accident separated me from
the drive to take the world by the throat. It helped me to
begin to shed some of my self-serving ways and let go of those
controls which hindered me from being gentle with others.
Since that began I've started to appreciate my capacity to share
myself with the people I care for. Perhaps the accident forced
a crack in the hard crust of my masculine ways and allowed
the dormant feminine life to flower through.

The example of that developing capacity which is dearest
to me is also the one I cherish as an occasion when I came
close to getting it right as a father.

It happened this way. My eldest son, David, had hung on
academically into his final year at school. With a somewhat
nervous gaze he announced he wanted to leave school and
Melbourne to go to Adelaide for awhile to gather some time
and personal territory. A big decision for a seventeen year-
old. Although quite clever with maths and symbols, he was
gradually becoming undermined by the heavily verbal
orientation of the essays and assignments.

As he talked in his hesitant way, I thought no-one should
be forced to become as unhappy at school as he was. And
I was impressed with the simple strength of his decision. The
HSC English topic that year had been Self-Identity which had
stimulated his thoughts and convictions on his own behalf.

I had no doubts that his plan was right for him and any advice or opposition would have been inappropriate. My job was to assist his decision in ways which ensured that his trip would be as safe and settled as it could be. A quick phone call to a friend set up safe accommodation, and a smooth car trip across to Adelaide and a weekend together allowed us time to talk and keep all doors open.

In three days he had a job, in three months he was back in Melbourne with the family, and the following year he was happily enrolled in a tertiary course of his choice. While he was away he sent me a card with a quote, 'A dad is someone who helps his son along the path he chooses, even when the path is strange'.

My recovery made me appreciate that gentleness is not weakness. One can break a concrete path with a noisy violent jackhammer. But a small plant can do it with nothing more than its delicate will to live.

One upsetting consequence of having my body smashed has been that I now have a real terror of violence. Before the accident I was physically rather fearless. That recklessness has changed completely. Any suggestion or even vague possibility of an involvement with physical blows will see me slide away. It isn't just a simple need for me to avoid physical conflict: it is a consuming instinct to protect myself against further injury. There are times when I pass or see violence when I quite unashamedly want to arm myself for my own protection. I have a narrow-eyed suspicion which puts me on guard. People who have been assaulted feel the same need, and perhaps many women.

During recovery, and particularly through that period when I felt the changes gaining their strength, I was aware that I was uncovering a larger part of the spectrum of sensibilities which overlaps between men and women. For the most part this involved me revealing some of the gentler female-associated values. I not only welcomed this 'gender drift' but was overjoyed by the changes—particularly as many of them have endured. And I was aware that the new rhythms and cycles of life I was appreciating were in strong contrast to the linear, direct, hierarchial patterns I had accepted previously.

Because of the influence and example of my mother I have never regarded women as weak in any way. My mother never indulged me, and while I can't speak to the truth of the quip 'behind every male chauvinist there is an over-indulgent mother', I can say that the power of female example is more telling than tokenism or slogans. It has always been strong and self-reliant women who have attracted me, and my deepest friendships have been with women who have these qualities.

And yet there was an aspect of my recovery which suggested that at one point invalidism and feminism could intersect.

As a relatively strong, tall and heavy male I had little fear of physical exposure. I could walk the streets alone at night, jog in the park at any hour, and sleep safely anywhere with doors and windows unlocked. But as a physically incapacitated male, in bed, in a wheelchair or on crutches, I experienced some of the safety fears which many women feel: of violence; of being unable to protect myself—even against five year-olds with pushers; of dependence on others for basic physical safety; and of the psychological depletion which any incessant fear can cause.

Children who are unprotected from physical intimidation, some women and anyone who has significant physical disabilities—particularly if that disability has been caused by some sort of assault—all can share a sense of sustained apprehension for their vulnerability against the possibility of force.

Just as an individual who has never had children cannot be aware of the incessant demand on parents' emotional resources that the never-ending vigilence for their safety creates, it is also difficult for physically competent men to appreciate the sense of physical discomfort and danger which women feel in many situations. Injured men begin to understand.

I need to say something about the years immediately before the accident to help me explain how and why the axis of my life turned. While it certainly was a help to my recovery that I was in a fit condition when I was struck, I'm uncertain why those years had been used so exclusively for athletic and physical activities.

In the earlier decades I'd been too consumed with cerebral challenges which produced tangible symbols of achievement to be bothered with exercise. Thinking back, I realised that I needed some relief from the consuming personal work of the previous decade. And I was tired of words: thousands and thousands had been written in articles and books and just as many had been spoken in lectures and formal talks. Words had become everything. I began to hear them echoing before they'd been written or delivered. Thoughts, ideas, interests, imaginings, discussions, arguments and theories seemed to resound even in my sleep.

The joy of athletic pursuits was that they were silent expressions of personal effort and were without worry. The only record they left was the private pleasure of having experienced something satisfying. Because this joy was a true extension of my consuming interests, I lost the weary feeling that I was a 'human doing' and regained the sense that I was a 'human being'. And some of my athletic activities, like running and especially windsurfing, were wonderfully private. I remember once returning from a sail across the bay, dropping the sail near Faulkner beacon, and, sitting close to the shipping lanes, I looked back up to the city and shouted, 'Try and get me with a telephone now!' The seagulls sitting on the beacon shook their heads.

In retrospect, it was remarkable how suddenly and completely my personal preoccupations turned from verbal to physical activities. I stopped reading almost overnight and pushed aside creative writing absolutely. Perhaps not so remarkable for a compulsive personality.

The strength and fitness which came from those athletic years undoubtedly helped my survival. But later on, as I looked back over the decade and remembered the written and spoken words it had created, I began to feel disappointed that the creative pause had been so long.

The accident served as a warning against extremes in my life and asked me to harmonise things better: to develop a balanced life which included physical, mental, emotional and spiritual dimensions. It did more than ask, it directed, because physical pursuits were no longer possible in the areas I had enjoyed. I couldn't run; windsurfing produced dangerous cramps, and squash caused further damage to my ankles. I began to cycle and walk with great pleasure because both activities offered the enchanting opportunity for simple observation.

I began to understand that compulsive behaviour in any form meant a return to my old self-damaging ways. I tried to avoid the pursuit of anything which involved unbalanced single-mindedness. It's true that my earlier approach had brought some rewards but they had been won at the price of a disjointed, relentless and destructive life.

At first, this tempered approach to life produced feelings of superficiality: I was doing many things in a more balanced way but without any sense of deep achievement. This feeling of trivialness worried me until I realised that to live as intensely and harmoniously as I could in the present moment—the only moment that I had available—was all I could do. Gradually, the individual moments of fulfillment began to add up to days of balance and happiness which were not without their personal productivity. These achievements were no less valuable because they had been won through a saner approach to living.

It would be a complete waste of time for me to wonder whether I would have been brought to this point of peaceful co-existence with myself as quickly, if at all, had it not been for the pause enforced by the accident. In part, recovery involved regaining some control and not being quite so emotionally reactive. And as I began to walk again in the streets, shopping, chatting, going to films and visiting friends, responses got better. I didn't over-react to innocent incidents which previously had me in alternating binges of moody silence or shouting.

Occasionally there were moments of unexpected and overwhelming tenderness. They involved times when, by chance, I met someone in the street or shops who was valued and dear to me. I had a rush of feeling that had I died they would have been lost. I wonder if they understood why I embraced them with such desperation. If those clumsy actions puzzled them I can only plead that the randomness of our meeting robbed me of any chance to prepare a moderate emotional response. I had to hug what they meant to me.

But meeting people was sometimes a source of confusion because time played tricks with me. Seven or eight months went missing. I was in a small time warp: whenever I said 'recently' it translated to 'a year ago' in ordinary time. When I began to meet people again, I realised that 'recovery time' was measured on a different clock.

I met a friend in the street and asked, 'How is your baby?'

'I have two now,' she replied.

A whole season was subtracted from the sporting calendar and two or three seasons from the year. It seemed to go from early autumn to late spring. One doesn't think of seasons being stolen. Whenever I recalled an event related to work I was always a year out. Released prisoners will understand what I'm trying to say.

I tried to make excuses for my vagueness but that was unnecessary. Most people understood from my appearance that something had happened to me. They all commented how tired I looked. What was missing was the shine in my eyes. That disturbed me more than the black rings beneath them.

One of the reasons for my weariness was my inability to sleep soundly. There is an important stage in the drift down to sleep. It comes when the mind manages to clear itself of the cares of the day and settles towards slumber. This dusk of thought is a fragile place which dislikes disruptions; and anything which damages its twilight peace causes a sluggish sort of irritation from which it is difficult to return to a sleepy state. Each night as I eased myself towards this place, a noise which had been partially masked by the competing sounds of a busy day began to unwind itself. It was a cicada-like screech, rasping like a clumsy attempt to tune a short wave radio. It is called tinnitus. It can be caused by a bomb exploding near a head or other trauma. It prevents rest. It hinders sleep. It reminds me of the impact. It is like the high-pitched hum in the head of chronic tiredness.

Seven years after the accident it is still sounding its siren. I wish it were gone. It invades all the purely private moments of my life when quietness should be my mate: before sleep, during meditation, during intimacy and when trying to release my imagination.

I had to take some tablets to sleep in the early months because without them even shallow rest was a struggle. They seemed innocuous and that's what made them so sinister. I woke up without any apparent side effects. But during the day the edge seemed to be missing from everything. Vibrance had been subtracted from the world. When I stopped taking them a darkness gathered over my spirits, but then gradually there was a wonderful clearing. The clouds seemed to separate in my mind and a warm light brought back a clarity to the world.

These days if my patients' moods are low I ask them to

consider setting aside sleeping pills, sugar, cigarettes and coffee for a week and if they feel more alive to leave them alone for longer.

There was one very peculiar consequence of the accident which was unusual and intriguing. I lost the capacity for the gut-wrenching fear I had experienced when trapped in my petrol splashed car. It was almost as though the intensity of the fear of dying killed my capacity to experience it again. Perhaps some sorts of bravery are expressions of that emptiness. I wondered if the body had only one huge reserve of that sort of self-preserving fear which burned itself out with use.

The possibility of that loss was revealed to me one day after I'd returned to work. Six of us were in a lift which suddenly went into a free fall for two or three floors before the safety clamps gripped it to a knee-buckling halt. My co-passengers were ashen. Four of them either wet themselves or retched. And I just stood there without either a visceral sensation or a change to my pulse rate—a nonhuman detachment. My whole being seemed to have developed an immunity to the deep fear experienced when one directly faces death. When I arrived in the office someone asked, 'Why the wry smile?'

'Oh nothing,' I lied truthfully.

How does one accept a 'benefit' brought by a loss? Does a man who loses a leg feel satisfied because he can never break it? I sat down at my desk and felt chilled by the awareness that my capacity for that sort of fear was gone. It was like losing the capacity to feel physical pain: superficially it might feel good until one realises that the sensation of pain had been evolved to protect us from injury or warn us about illness. Pain is protective and so is fear. To lose either is to reduce one's chances of survival.

It was years before I regained an appropriate sense of fear at moments of real danger. It happened when a water cooling valve on my car stuck and caused the engine to overheat and cut out, taking with it the power brakes and steering. It happened as I was on a five kilometre descent at speed in busy traffic on a narrow roadway. That peril which was drawn out over two minutes, produced a return of real fear.

As I began to feel more alive I recovered my dissatisfaction with cosy ease. It made me want to produce something which justified the energies I spent. There is nothing like a good dose of near death to emphasize our frailty. The thought of being a faceless passenger on the planet who left no grand work didn't bother me. What unsettled me was the feeling that committed human effort which consumed enormous amounts of personal energy could dissipate without making a contribution to a shape somewhere. I wanted to believe that something should feel and respond to the effort. Something should change.

It was enforced rest which provided the insight to realise that working in the Health Department public service, apart from rare occasions, provided little real chance to make meaningful change. Instead, it was producing progressive personal numbness, bluntness and despair. I was grateful that the accident prevented the effects of a draining job from becoming a way of life.

19
WORK

To get the whole world out of bed
And washed, and dressed, and warmed and fed,
To work, and back to bed again,
Believe me, Saul, costs worlds of pain.

John Masefield

I went back to work too early. Physicians should not try to heal themselves or ignore the guidance of others who know. I tried to seize at a symbol of recovery and paid the penalty of adding to my existing recovery tasks the job of trying to convince others and myself that I could manage something that was beyond both my capacities and interest. I should have protected myself. The act of returning to work announced to everyone that I was fit and competent to cope with all the demands of the job.

It's true that my colleagues tried to make allowances for me during the first weeks, but after that it was a whirlpool of progressive worries where my availability was a sufficient signal for others to call on my capacities in the way they had before I was injured.

During those early weeks following my return to part-time work I was strengthened by the goodness of my work colleagues and their wish for me to regain health. But I was appalled by the inefficiency of the work—the emptiness of it all. It seemed like a masquerade of political pragmatism posturing as true purpose.

I looked in disbelief at the stagnation. So little had moved;

but I had, away from it all. Files on my desk were still waiting for resource decisions on submissions for additional services; correspondence was still shuttling between departments without any responsibility being accepted, and all sorts of interdepartmental games were in progress whose single objective seemed to be an attempt to change the name of everything and the nature of nothing. Personnel were being shifted while overall departmental performance deteriorated. I could no longer justify spending my vocational efforts on futility and pretence.

The timing of my heedless return to work was a mistake. Some women and men who occupy what are regarded as 'positions of responsibility' don't always manage this return well after a major illness. Even fewer are willing to admit that their return was a mistake because it is in the nature of people who thrive on achievement to fear failure and use the habit of self-justification instead of honesty. These days I know that any temporary convenience of dishonesty does not offset the weariness produced by the inevitable accompanying self-deception. It just isn't worth the bother. The shortest distance between two emotional points is the truth. In terms of simple emotional effort it became easier for me to be honest and far easier to be forthright when I accepted that my personal relevance was not determined solely by my public performance, especially my performance at work.

But at the time I returned to work I felt that there were so many things I needed to prove or rather reprove, and such a desire to show everyone that my powers and potency were still intact. It was one of the worst mistakes I have made in my life and no-one was responsible but myself. And it was as sad as it was unnecessary.

I ignored the warnings of others who could see that I was limping into a vocational swamp. I neglected the obvious consequences: I failed to heed the advice I had given to so many of my own patients who had been in the same position. And worst of all, I persisted even when I knew things were wrong, feeling, pathetically, that to surrender from work was like failing to report for duty.

The job I returned to at the State Health Department was a difficult one, even for a fully fit person. It involved responsibility for the coordination of all rehabilitation and aged care services across the state, requiring public exposure and participation in a range of visits, meetings, delegations and staff discussions. I had to be there to talk, listen, respond, balance, arbitrate, assess and conclude. And all this at a time when I wanted minimal human contact. At that stage of my recovery I also disliked the extra demands created by uncertainty, something I normally enjoyed. But the job did not permit me to timetable stress points in an orderly way. They came as they pleased, unwanted and unwelcome visitors.

It was always worse in the afternoon. Whenever I went against my instinct not to attend meetings or functions after three pm when I was exhausted, I was made to regret the consequences.

Previously, one of the most enjoyable parts of the job had been visiting rural facilities. Country people were welcoming and many of their hospitals had a homely spirit which was missing from some of their urban counterparts. But the injuries meant I could not endure long drives. I was clamped to the city, struggling to reach a level of performance who no-one, apart from myself, expected me to achieve at that time, and in a job whose relevance to the wellbeing of elderly or disabled people seemed progressively more limited as a result of government 'action'.

At that time, the State Health Department was being restructured. At least that was the administrative name for it. Rather, in the eyes of many who left, it was undergoing a mutation which produced bureaucratic deformities, spitefulness, intimidation, vocational cannibalism and an environment where virtually all principles of personnel management seemed to be ignored or violated. It was the plague of the takeover. Normally, I would have enjoyed a professional joust, defending good but gentler colleagues and counter-punching vocational bullies. But my exhaustion and low endurance left me with no base from which to launch an attack and no defence or escape from spiteful snipes. After three months back at work my spirit was completely drained. I began to feel ill each time I climbed into the car to do another day's battle.

Soon I began to doubt that the job was a suitable vocational vehicle for my range of professional abilities. I knew I wanted to leave pure administration and return to a job which offered the more fulfilling opportunities of doctor-patient contact. That move was not an option I could undertake with depleted internal resources. How could I subject myself to the scrutiny of an interview and undertake the tasks of a new job when I hardly had the emotional energy required to face the day? And how could I return to surgery with ankles that could not support me standing comfortably for more than an hour?

My distorted thinking told me that I had to return to my current job and reprove myself so that I would be a worthy contender for any future jobs. It was an unnecessary, insane and almost ruinous decision from which I was rescued by an unexpected and direct invitation to accept just the sort of position I was seeking. The offer—which I accepted—was for the Medical Directorship at Hampton Rehabilitation Hospital.

I have now lived a life of complete vocational fulfillment for the past six years at the place where I had previously been a patient for seven months. The same examination couches and the same equipment I used and the same pool and gymnasium I worked in are now occupied by my current patients.

20
REMINDERS

Memory fades, must the remembered
Perishing be?

Walter De La Mare

The reminders came unexpectedly, no matter how hard I tried
to get on with other things. There were so many of them,
the road toll in the papers, an accident on the radio news,
an advertisement directed towards reducing road deaths, a
passerby in a wheelchair, a smash on the other side of the
road, or the gut-wrenching sound of screeching tires. And the
dreams of drowning in fire. These days most of them are easy
to deflect. One or two still remain but even they are fading.
I'm grateful I have been given the time to cope with these
sources of pain. Some of them are still associated with feelings
of distress.

Why, for instance, do the road death statistics need to
be published repeatedly in the daily papers? No other cause
of death intrudes in this way. We don't see, 'Heart attack
toll: this year, 4,562; last year, 4,321'. Even for sudden deaths
due to fires, floods or earthquakes, we get the blunt statistics
for a few weeks and then they reappear only on anniversaries.

What purpose do these macabre road-toll score-boards
achieve? Do they make passengers or pedestrians better drivers?
Do they make drunks stop drinking? Do they improve the car
control of people who are already good drivers but who have
little protection against the reckless road barbarians who run

through red lights and speed? Would they prevent that significant number of single car collisions into trees or poles which are not accidents but clearly self destruction?

No. Their major impact is to cause repeated ulcerating distress to the relatives of those who died, and to provide painful memories for those who have survived with their bodies broken. They are a violent, unhelpful and unnecessary intrusion.

I was grateful to be spared the wretched guilt suffered by those who had injured or killed loved ones, friends or strangers—through culpable driving. They had to make recoveries I was grateful to be spared and they had to endure the inquisitorial aspects of convictions I only had to witness. The effects of scheduled court appearances on some of my co-patients were devastating. Those who survived managed by letting go of the past and living each day the best they could. Whatever they had done, I admired their courage. They were battling on three simultaneous fronts of physical, emotional and moral damage while I struggled with two.

I haven't met a single patient who has been involved with an accident or assault who has expressed anything but an intense dislike at having to fill out any official documents or declarations about their accident. But it goes deeper than that. Inquiries from police, insurance companies or work agencies filled me with indignation and anxiety. At the time in recovery when all my energies were trying to look forward, an enforced re-run of all the events I was trying to forget was always distressing. The worst were the legal documents which needed to be completed with details of the accident and injuries, even though it was in my interest to fill them out.

When an accident victim is caught up in an adversarial legal action, it can be as harrowing as the initial accident, in spite of being the innocent and injured party who stands to benefit from the proceedings. If such actions go to court, the experience can be totally draining and even humiliating. One of my co-patients was asked to strip to show a jury his injuries.

I know of many patients, myself included, who had very few fearful dreams during their stay in hospital and subsequent recovery, but who lost a lot of sleep when the legal machine began to mince them. Everyone should give early consideration to settling out of court as soon as possible.

Even though the legal process was trying, most of the lawyers and police I had to deal with were very decent people, especially the policeman who came to interview me. I was not looking forward to his arrival in the ward, and when he came I dreaded the anticipated conversation because I feared it would tear at the tissue-thin healing of my wounds. It didn't happen that way. In spite of his newness to the task, he managed to delicately balance sensitive concern with essential cross-questioning about the circumstances of the accident in a way which won my appreciation. In fact, he was one of the most considerate professionals I had to face during the whole long pilgrimage and is the reason why I have always acknowledged policemen with courtesy.

But what a squalid place a county court is. What an unworthy place for something as grand as the hearing against the chap who drove the truck which hit me. Perhaps not. The grime, the peeling paint, the weariness of the building, the scars on the lino and the cold, diminishing austerity all signified elements in my recovery.

At this trial I remained standing on my crutches, leaning against the court wall, too wasted for vengeance, too tired for victory.

The truck driver mumbled something about pleading guilty to driving through a red light and was fined $200 and banned from driving for half a year. If he saw the crushed contents of my car in his dreams he has had sentence enough. He didn't set out to kill me that morning, and almost all of us have driven through a red light at some time.

The court was concerned only with traffic laws, the human was of interest only if dead. Or so they said at the police station.

A bit later on, when all the plasters had gone, and some strength was returning to my legs, I was driving in busy traffic and had to brake suddenly. My whole body was held fast by the grip of the seat belt and I felt as though someone had taken a six inch wide strap and struck me across my body, along a band which covered the dislocations and rib fractures from my right shoulder to the left side of my chest. Every muscle, joint, ligament and bone along that line which had received the full force of the accident, screamed again. I stopped the car and rested across the steering wheel until the pain became manageable. Shaking and sweating with relief, I knew that the force borne by the seat belt on my chest on the day of the accident had saved my head from being smashed into salivating stupidity.

Of all the things for which I feel a sense of gratitude none is greater than to have been spared a head injury.

'Lost head, lost human,' said the mother of a brain damaged son who was attending a public meeting I was chairing recently on head injury. I still get emotional about the profound loss caused by injuries to the brain. The victim loses who they are. The family loses who they were. The world loses who they could have been.

There can be nobility and courage in the face of adversity— and God really does know how much the parents who care for brain damaged children show these qualities—but nothing good comes from brain damage. And it is nearly always the mother and father who pick up the burden. Friends visit for a few weeks, special friends for a few months, family members for a few years. But Mum and Dad do it for life.

'The worst thing,' said one of the fathers, 'is that our boy is now alone, apart from us. None of the old friends visit any more. As soon as it became clear he was not going to be normal. If you want to get the message through to young people, tell them they will be without a friend in six months after they have a head injury.'

I need to say again my gratitude at being spared a damaged brain is unqualified.

One of the greatest reminders of the accident is also something which arouses feelings of fury. It happens each time I see someone driving with wilful recklessness—speeding, swerving over the lanes and cutting across other drivers. Instead of simply being grateful that my life is not in the sort of chaos which requires that sort of driving, it takes every bit of my self-control not to chase after them and blast them. No. It's worse than that. I actually feel quite murderous. If I had a car cannon I would explode them from the road. If I had rotating blades, I would carve their car like a can opener.

I wish there was a special police phone line which I could ring to give them the time, location and car details of dangerous drivers. It might help prevent some double damage: to their lives and my sanity.

Recently I was driving behind a woman who, in the space of 800 metres, broke virtually every existing traffic law.

'Congratulations,' I said to her with open sarcasm as our cars met at the next traffic lights.

'Why?' she asked with a mock smile as her son lent forward beside her.

'Because you've just endangered twenty people's lives in thirty seconds.'

'Why don't you go home and have a nice calming drink,' she said, trying to bait me.

'And why don't you come down to my hospital and see the head-injured patients of your son's age,' I said bluntly.

The second time I passed through the smash intersection after the accident was not premeditated. I was just travelling to visit a friend. The red light stopped me and I looked across at the spot wondering if I would find any broken bits still there, or find where much of my living energy had gone, or where it could have stopped forever. It was a very long, unblinking, hollow look.

21
LATE RECOVERY

Patiently adjust, amend, and heal.

Thomas Hardy

Eventually, recovery started to become harmonious. In the early
months it was like an orchestra tuning up with the physical,
emotional and spiritual elements of life scratching their own
unconducted, untuned sounds. Then the time came when I
felt ready to be tapped into a tune. Different parts started
playing together and I slowly began to feel the strength of
a united wellbeing. As Oliver Sacks observed, 'Every disease
is a musical problem, every cure a musical solution'. At that
time I had no doubts I was truly recovering and when people
said, 'You look well,' I replied openly, 'Yes, thank you, I am
feeling well'.

The good things which followed the accident happened
gradually. One of the most important was the ease with which
I reduced my everyday expectations. I had to reduce them
in relation to my physical abilities but I also realised that in
my general life all expectations tended to obscure what really
existed. In my case expectations were presumptuous and
uncharitable to others because they imposed a sense of what
ought to be rather than an acceptance of what was. As I
mentioned earlier, some of the most rewarding benefits of this
realisation involved the children, but they also involved a kinder
approach to myself and others.

People with overbearing expectations are always in the way of themselves and others. They erase what is and would rather possess a touched-up picture than touch the real thing.

The accident put an end to my fundamental belief in the reliability of life. It brought a way of thinking where nothing could be taken for granted and nothing could be presumed. Everything was left to breathe and grow in its own way and in its own time. In the loveliest sense, I strived to have acceptance without expectations as my basic approach to all people and situations. This improved both my genuine human availability and my desire to see others embrace ways which were their choice, as with my eldest son's trip to South Australia. It was a letting go which provided the foundation for a richer peace of mind which was still two or three years away.

It was about the time that I began to feel stronger that the doctors confirmed I would need a further operation. A tendon graft was necessary to repair the damage done to my left leg and to enable me to use my ankle. The prospect of being enclosed in yet another plaster, raised doubts about my desire to go on with recovery. I felt as though I had experienced and contributed all I could and that I hadn't done anything to deserve this. For a short time I found the second round of operations more difficult to cope with than the earlier emergency surgery. I lacked the inclination or will to take up the challenge of my own wellbeing. Perhaps it was the treachery of summer that did it. The boiling days melted into the middle of autumn with me again imprisoned in plaster at the time of the first anniversary of the accident.

Fortunately, my spirits rallied quickly. In a way, the short strike of despondency was almost a memory reflex to the savage months of the previous year. I was being forced to relive something that had not been resolved. I took a dose of Emerson's essays and cured myself. His writings are a living therapy, full of spirit and strength, bursting with enthusiasm for the value and potential of each individual.

The reason for the later operation was obvious to me before anyone else acknowledged it. Physiotherapists were puzzled and surgeons doubtful. But rehabilitation medicine had taught me that there is a simple clinical principle which applies to a recovery from multiple injuries: unless there is a good reason, all injuries should progress and improve at the same rate. Clearly this was not the case with my left leg where all the muscles except one were regaining strength and bulk. And this muscle was an important source of strength to my foot. In its wasted state it struggled to assist the graded placement of my ankle with each step. Instead, the foot slapped into the floor or pavement as I walked.

This bulky muscle, which extends down alongside the sharp front edge of the shin bone to become a finger-thick tendon one can feel and see across the front of the ankle when it is flexed upwards, was wasted, and its tendon seemed to be missing. At first I thought the tendon may have been stuck to the bulk of healing bone beneath it at the fracture site, but as time went on and no muscle tendon could be felt on either side of the fracture area, I knew it had been severed by the smash.

I rang my orthopaedic surgeon, John Harris, who had done such a superb job fixing my fractures. 'That's a very rare injury, Tony,' he said. 'Very unusual. But come in and let me have a look at the leg next week.'

'Thanks John,' I said, appreciating his willingness to test what was surgically 'unusual' against my first class honour in anatomy and Francis Bacon's axiom that the patient has lived with his own body longer than anyone else.

I knew, for example, that it was not natural for the muscles which extended my toes to cramp helplessly because of the work they were doing to compensate for the missing muscle whose job it was to extend my ankle. Nor was it appropriate for the ball of my forefoot to crash into the floor with each step because the impact of my heel was unprotected against the effect of gravity on my body's weight.

'You're right,' he said with considerable clinical interest after examining my leg the following week.

I was soon ready for the operating theatre again, to fix the tendon and to remove the remaining screw from the right ankle at the same time.

William Wilson was the plastic surgeon involved with the tendon graft, taking the spare tendon of the remnant monkey muscle at the back of the calf and weaving it into graceful figures of eight to make up the defect. In the moment before I went under the anaesthetic I handed him a tiny rose which he wore during the operation. I should have given one to the anaesthetist too because my life depended more on his silent skills than it did on my surgeon's ability.

When I woke up, back in a dreaded plaster, Bill explained the difficulty and challenge he had encountered. 'Everything was stuck together with fibrous tissue right over the fracture site,' he said. 'I could see how the leg had been trying to use the muscle without a tendon to help it. Your efforts had fashioned the surrounding connective tissue into an ineffective strip of pseudotendon. It was fascinating to see the attempt at adaption.'

I wondered how many surgeons wished their patients had a detailed knowledge of the anatomy and physiology of their bodies so they could share their clinical findings. Bill seemed pleased to be able to discuss the details of his labours.

In common with all surgeons he was fascinated by the relationship between anatomical structure and applied function. 'I've done my best,' he said. 'But the rough bed of the graft didn't help me.'

His 'best' was excellent and eventually enabled me to regain thirty to forty per cent of the function in the muscle. The continuity of the tendon was restored, and with splendid physiotherapy and some effort on my part, the operation enabled me to get the tendon unstuck from its fibrous adhesions and mobile again. But the imperfect length meant that its mechanical action, which had been precisely developed by eons of human evolution, was a fraction wrong. That was enough to reduce its efficiency and prevent restoration of its full function.

As I watched the tendon working with perfect static contraction across the ankle when the toes were pointing down, but lax and ineffective when the ankle was drawn back, I was not filled with disappointment, but rather with awe and wonder at the marvellous integration and balance of our movements when our muscles and joints are working perfectly.

As soon as I got out of the plaster I worked in the water of the bay to improve the strength of the leg. For the second time I gained great strength from being near the sea during my recovery. Its vigour helped me to rest. The strength and surge of its endless energy seemed to accept the total responsibility for all other activity and left me nothing to do but watch in wonder. I loved the reliable rhythm of the waves thumping timelessly like nature's heartbeat.

This love is now a way of life. Today, there is no greater source of nourishment for my spirits than to stroll and sit by the ocean sea where its sounds speak of personal peace and solitude. The spray and the salt soak me warm and when the tides turn and touch the sand with a sculptor's skill, the edged patterns have cathedral beauty.

During recovery the sea helped to save my life. Now it is teaching me about delicacy. In the rock pools and in the lace foam of its breaking waves, in the changing shades of mauve, turquoise, aqua and pink, in the filamentous intricacy of its living structures—everywhere there is delicacy. Nothing else in my life has the sea's capacity to change and yet remain constant. It is a magnificent and reassuring mystery. It helps me to have faith that I have a place. And it has taught me about the other rhythms of nature.

The movement in atoms is elliptical, and so are the orbits in the universe. The largest and smallest elements in our lives have the ellipse as their guide. There is a message there for me which helps explain the rhythms of my emotions. They don't oscillate, they don't travel in parallel, they don't circle me evenly. Instead they do what all things in the universe do, they move in great loops towards me when I am regaining happinesss, accelerating when I am happy in the extreme, and then, as they move away, slowly stimulating sadness and occasionally even deep despondency.

The most reassuring thing about an ellipse is that its state is not steady but says 'this too will pass'. It reassures me that at those moments of remote stillness it is turning on an infinitely small moment from moving out to moving in. Like the time of the turning tide, the moments of dawn and dusk, or the drift from one season to the next, as with every pendulum in nature, there is also a tiny instant of stillness. I don't need to panic at this moment. It will turn and return.

One reward from the accident was quite unexpected. I lost that fuzzy feeling of apprehension I had experienced whenever life was going well. A vague sense of abstract anxiety had always partnered my happiness: the fear that it would not last and that something would come along and fiddle with my delight. Not only has that feeling gone, but now I am aware of why it has been replaced with a robust and enduring sense of joy.

Because my earlier happiness was based on events and people, it was always exposed and vulnerable to changes in those external elements. Following the accident, and having recovered the resolve for survival, I saw life in a cleaner light. My primary sense of contentment was no longer based on external directions but rather on an inner sense of gentle gladness which arose from a new and independent feeling of personal worth.

I had survived. With all the blemishes and credits in my make-up, I had been preserved—the being who was nowhere else in nature, who had never been before and never would be again—that messy richness which was me. I celebrated the truth that like all human beings I was unique, unprecedented and unrepeatable. My fundamental happiness, based on an appreciation of my tiny but clear position in the order of things, now remains steady regardless of whatever is going on around me.

The event which captured my recovery most comprehensively was a particular bike ride I did a year and a-half after the accident. It was special because it united my physical and emotional progress, and provided a contrast to the ragged approach to life I had taken in earlier years. After many purposeful months in the gymnasium and progressively longer training rides, I was ready to tackle a trip which loomed large in my mind—a bike ride to my mother-in-law's property at Emerald, sixty-five kilometres of hills and heart-power. Before the accident I had rushed into the challenge of this ride churning down the slopes at full pedal only to stall exhausted towards the top of the steepest incline and suffer the indignity of having to walk the bike to the summit.

This time it had to be different. I knew that my legs didn't have the strength and that my body lacked the endurance for a 'run against the clock'. So I set out at a manageable slower pace along the relatively flat sections of the city until I passed the VFL football ground on the outskirts of Melbourne where the hills began to demand my full attention. At that stage I picked up a wonderfully fluid rhythm in the pedals and with each push sounded a refrain in my brain: go slow—

let go, go slow—let go. I kept lowering the gears up the hills to maintain the beat and the steepness just melted in front of the wheels. What had been an unmanageable ordeal when attacked with my pre-accident 'fitness' became a smooth flow with a more careful approach.

I was thrilled when I arrived at Emerald. For the first time since the accident I had done something physically significant of which I had been incapable before the smash. It was a simple demonstration of the power of letting go and moving with the grain of the task. My whole body smiled and sang.

The experiences of the accident revealed in the most radiant way the rich colours of human kindness and generosity and the importance of friendship. On only one bitter occasion did they display human meanness, when, on my need to return to hospital for the tendon graft twelve months after the accident, an acquaintance knowingly sniped, 'Having another holiday?'

That remark was shaded by the goodness of those who wished me well throughout my whole recovery. They wrote, they called, they helped at home, they shouldered at work, and some directed their prayers and thoughts towards me. Big bits of healing energy came my way and I couldn't have survived without them.

The surgeons and the other staff helped to heal my bones but my friends encouraged the deepest healing. It was the unexpected expressions of friendship which supported me the most, when people provided a word or a gesture or a touch which transferred the energy of their wish for me to be well. Their tenderness was like having my spirit caressed.

Each of these friends who contributed so much to my survival now exists in the fabric of my life. Eventually, their goodness cradled me. They know who they are, the visitors, those who wrote letters, those who called to the house or who expressed delight when they saw me walking again in the streets. And now, seven years on, beyond the territory of recovery, it is almost impossible for me to express my debt and the affection I feel for them. I hope it is enough for them to know they are with me forever.

There is a difference between being a victim of an accident

and an accident victim. One is an event and the other a degrading process. When one's individual resources are completely spent, only friendship can change the direction of that degradation.

The experience of the accident has made me more observant of many things which I gazed past in earlier years. I see the physical toil of people struggling with disabilities. I notice the human frustration and pain in people's eyes. I am a brother to the fear and anger in their faces. And I am thrilled when I see hope and happiness returning to their lives.

22
CROSSROAD

We are all patched people

The accident was not a starting point. It was a punctuation mark in the sentence of my existence, influenced by all the previous chapters and affecting all the pages which have followed. It's hard to know the magnitude of its impact, whether it altered only the way the story was to be told or whether it forced a real change to the plot. At the time, it felt as though the whole book had been burned.

Today it seems like a mischievous act of the fates, the way small boys can twist a country road sign causing a traveller to lose direction, but ultimately to be enriched by the diversion.

Before the accident I had never really thought about my relationship with roads. In a variety of ways, large proportions of our lives are involved with streets, routes, freeways, highways, crossings, junctions and intersections. When I do a free association with the word 'road', my immediate responses include 'car', 'pollution', 'laws', 'danger', 'accident', 'toll', and 'deaths'. We even call some of them 'arterials' or 'bypasses'. In earlier, more sedate times this word association might have produced 'travel', 'coach', 'adventure', 'journey', 'trip', or 'holiday'. Our present-day involvement with roads is one of increasing concern, decreasing utility and vanishing pleasure.

Roads also form part of the psychological strata along which our individual lives have travelled. During my life I seem to have had an adventurous relationship with them. As a small boy there were two memorably bruising encounters which I had with both vehicles and male unfairness.

On one occasion, as a free-wheeling nine year-old, I was pedalling down Motherwell Street when the chain of my bike started to rub on the guard. I looked down, hoping to make some running repairs and rode straight into the back of a stationary baker's cart. Over the handlebars I went, my somersault cushioned by the wooden shelves and soft loaves which tumbled over me as the horse bolted half a mile down the street with me still in the back of the cart. The baker showed no interest at all in the bent front forks of my bike— instead he tried to fashion my ears the same way.

The second event was not only more dangerous but also more fiercely unfair. I was cycling down the Williams Road hill, coming back from my paper selling corner on Toorak Road, when a driver opened the door of his parked car right in front of me. I swerved quickly but the corner of the door clipped my leg and sent me careering across the road while the unsold papers went flying into the sky like kites and the money from my leather shoulder bag scattered like marbles as I slid into the curb on the opposite side of the road. With bleeding knees and rasped knuckles I stood up shaking and shouted, 'You stupid man!'

He walked over, belted me across the head, strolled back to his car, and drove away.

I sat down on the gutter. There are some things which happen to ten year-old boys that they don't tell their mothers. Especially when there is no old man around to act as a protector.

My recovery has been an intensely personal experience. The private nature of the ordeal was not simply a result of the obvious event in that it was my body which was damaged. It was also a profoundly isolating experience, partly because the man who was involved was damaged before the accident happened, creating a person who did not encourage intimacy and who may have produced feelings of awe and even fear in those who had a wish to be close to him. And partly because the additional damage produced a feeling inside his soul that he was no longer the person he had been and that the new creature initially had even less emotional cohesion than his pre-accident self.

Almost without exception, these factors united to produce a situation where I felt isolated and alone for the whole period of recovery. Strangely, it was only after I had begun to heal my spirits that I was able to allow my family and other loved ones to get closer and to help me. One of the worst pains produced by the accident was the realisation that the support and friendship I needed during the hardest parts of recovery were unavailable, unrecognised, unwanted or unembraced.

Today, when I read this account of my recovery it feels mysterious and incomplete. People seem to be missing from it. But because of my sense of separateness at the time, that was the reality. I cannot pretend it was otherwise with accounts of folksy friendships and an easy love between me and my family or close friends, without betraying the experience. I cannot describe my recovery with a boy scout buoyancy or a happy-ever-after ending without denying the truth of the experience. One cannot light a candle to study darkness. I'd rather be disliked for revealing what I truly experienced than liked for some pretense.

I can't be certain how common is the deep sense of isolation among those who have suffered significant physical or emotional damage. The common soul I share with others—my patients, their families, my colleagues and friends—whispers to me that it is the truth.

Just as recovery was itself painfully difficult, it has not been easy for me to write about this serious and hurtful experience. It was an unrelenting ordeal; and it is hard to make despair sound engaging.

Humour had always been a help to me to soften what I needed to say or cover a discomfort. It could also be genuinely engaging and funny. Losing that sense of fun during recovery eliminated an important source of support which could have helped release me from the fearful seriousness of it all. But life was very sombre during recovery. The playful audacity which could have prevented me from taking things too seriously was missing. I know my recollections of the experience of the accident sadly reflect that loss.

The accident marked a crossroad in an untidy life. I have tried to make sure that the story has not been written by the limited skeleton of my professional self but rather by a blemished total being who has tried to be open. In a similar way, my story attempts to reveal how a *person*, and not just a *body*, recovers following major injury.

Today, from the steady perspective of seven years on, some things are clear. Physical recovery and its associated therapeutic supports are not the main problem: you heal what you can and you adapt to or accept the rest. But it's not that simple in the emotional, spiritual and psychological areas. From the deeper parts of a damaged person's being, the heart and soul can be dumped in the casualty department of life and languish there neglected while all around the busy world of physical resuscitation efficiently goes on.

I survived because the physical systems of support in intensive care, the operating theatres and the wards were perfectly tuned to assist the disruptions to my metabolism, circulation and general physiology. Machines, monitors and techniques had been evolved to a state of precise efficiency just like a perfectly adapted organism. Perhaps a few decades ago when they were primitive and imperfect, my injuries would have caused death, or survival as something less than human.

Technology now ensures physical recovery for many who would have died. But having survived severe damage, where is the therapeutic equivalent of intensive care units for the emotional wounds which can leech themselves onto a lacerated body? Where is the counterpart of the intensive care department for dismembered human feelings? They simply don't exist or are as rudimentary as eighteenth century blood-letting.

The reality is this: major physical injuries sustained through motor accidents, industrial mishaps, explosions, burns, war damage, civilian assaults, massacres, or natural disasters are usually well managed. This is also true of a large number of less dramatic cases, including infectious diseases, difficult pregnancies, diabetic management, and endocrine, kidney, liver and heart conditions. This physiological efficiency ensures that the physically damaged will survive, but with their associated spiritual and emotional contusions often unrevealed, undiagnosed and untreated. Have we understood that the spirit must accompany and assist this retrieval?

Frequently, people use masculine bravado or feminine forbearance to shrug off such damage and go it alone with brittle self-sufficiency. In many cases—as in mine—this denial can be emotionally disastrous. During the months of physical improvement where does an individual go to find an intensive care unit for this emerging deeper psychological damage? There isn't a place and probably never can be a comprehensive service which puts together the inner pieces.

My experience of recovery and the contact I have had with my own patients in subsequent years indicate that the necessary ingredients of an emotional support intensive care unit will vary with each individual and with the particular time in recovery. There are no single or simple answers and this is not an attempt to provide them. Rather, it is a plea for an increased awareness among both treating staff and patient relatives to appreciate some of the factors involved in this challenge. They include a reduction in the patient's single-minded drive to be self-sufficient; the humility to say, 'I need help'; the courage to admit to emotional pain, and the strength to do the things of life differently. Appropriate support requires that 'the arm of understanding' is offered by sensitive friends or by those who have previously experienced similar damage. Occasionally it can be provided by those professional counsellors who have skills to assist personal emergencies or who can reveal options for different ways of managing private pain.

For my own part I have learnt how to cry and how to call out when the pain becomes unbearable. No longer does the brave little boy need to conceal how much things can hurt—like the time in the headmaster's office in sixth grade.

Top of the class I was, and, unknown to me, set to receive a prize of ten pounds donated by the local grocer, as well as the usual speech day certificate. I knew Mum had to be at work in the kitchens of the Alfred Hospital during the Friday afternoon of the presentation, and, with no other existing parents or relatives to attend, I did what any self-respecting twelve year-old would do and went to the railway embankment to watch the trains go by.

I was summoned to the headmaster's office on the following Monday morning with an imperious demand for me to explain my absence and my rudeness. At that time, in 1952, I was the only kid in the class who didn't have a Dad and one of the very few whose mother had to work. My mute response to his towering demand for an explanation was interpreted as further evidence of my 'unacceptable attitude'. I tried to burn him with my stare as he dressed me down and demanded that I go to the grocer's shop to apologise and, if I was lucky, to collect my prize.

The grocer was fairly reasonable and asked me what I planned to spend it on. 'Use it for a book,' I said smiling.

The next Saturday I went to the horse races at Caulfield, jumped the fence from the path to the flat and climbed into the Guineas stand. The 'Books' and I had a mighty battle for that ten pounds during the rest of the day.

I hardly ever cried during my childhood. They were wasted years in the apprenticeship of being able to express emotions openly. Occasionally, even today, the old orphaned thoughts of the memory of some of those moments come back to remind me of that waste. Today my professional and personal activities against waste of any sort, especially the waste of human spirit or ability, are the most important aspects of my life.

In the years since the accident each time the calendar turns to 12 April, I feel the need to be still and quiet and to spend some time alone.

There is one person who must always remember the anniversary of the accident. It's not a celebration. It is a moment of eerie stillness, as in the seconds following the smash. It is like the feeling one has looking at the gravestone of someone who has died in their youth.

There came a time in my recovery when I knew I would never be the same again. When I reached that stage I knew I had to accept the differences and begin to appreciate that the changes could help me forwards. Although my public humour and irreverence have returned, a core of sorrow remains and it can't be shifted.

The journey continues quietly. Beginning again cannot mean living the same life twice. What was, has changed, and whatever is, will change.